T0061966

The Journey of a Caribbean Writer

THE
SEAGULL
LIBRARY OF
FRENCH
LITERATURE

INDIA

This work is published with the support of
Institut français en Inde – Embassy of France in India

Seagull Books, 2020

Original texts © Maryse Condé
English translation © Richard Philcox, 2014

First published in English translation by Seagull Books, 2014

ISBN   978 0 8574 2 755 7

British Library Cataloguing-in-Publication Data
A catalogue record for this book is available from the British Library.

Typeset by Seagull Books, Calcutta, India
Printed and bound by WordsWorth India, New Delhi, India

CONTENTS

What Is a Caribbean Writer?

A few years ago, Martinican poet Monchoachi raised the question: 'Where is the Caribbean? Where does it start and where does it end?'[1] The question is to the point and by no means trivial. Immigration has always been a major characteristic of our islands. At the beginning of the twentieth century, hundreds of thousands of Jamaicans, Trinidadians, Barbadians as well as Guadeloupeans and Martinicans rushed to dig the Panama Canal. They would pay with their lives for this technical feat, this marvel that split the world in two, and would die buried in the mud of Gatun. Marcus Garvey, on a visit to the region in 1930, saw for himself the immense misery of his fellow countrymen and thought up the idea of a massive return to the lost continent, Mother Africa.

I happen to have a photo which is very dear to me that dates even further back, to 1924. Taken on Ellis Island, the point of entry for immigrants to the USA, it shows a group of pretty, young Antillean women, bedecked with Creole jewellery, gold chokers, earrings and bracelets and dressed in their best Creole costume, having made it through the triple barrier of medical, police and customs inspection,

Originally published as 'Qu'est-ce qu'un Caribéen? *A fortiori*, qu'est-ce qu'un écrivain Caribéen?' in *Presence Francophone* 72 (2009): 162.

1 See Monchoachi, *La case où se tient la lune* (Bordeaux: William Blake and Co., 2002).

smiling at their future. Where were they going, I have often asked myself. Without a man at their side, were they in fact coming to their fiancés, husbands or families? What work had they come to do? Were they about to lose themselves in the American mirage? Or seek the American dream, so often illusory?

Closer to our time, we know all too well of the Cubans, Puerto Ricans, Dominicans, Balseros and boat people immigrating to Florida in every possible and imaginable way. Victims of their repeating dictatorships as well as their dysfunctional society, the Haitians flee into exile just about everywhere, be it Europe, Canada or the USA, whereas countless English-speaking people of the Caribbean continue to migrate to the UK. Those who are born and grow up there go by the convenient but somewhat mysterious term of 'Black British'. As for the 'French' islands, the BUMIDOM (Bureau pour le Développement des Migrations dans les Départements d'Outremer) certainly represented a milestone in the history of migration. Created by Michel Debré soon after the Algerian War in order to compensate for a labour shortage in France, it was the Beast, to paraphrase Simone Schwarz-Bart,[2] which swallowed the sun of thousands of men and women. Regurgitating in due course and place the Second Generations, it damaged for ever the contours of Antillean identity.

In recent years the Caribbean has swarmed and mushroomed in every direction. It has become a shapeless, elephantine place that takes on every name possible. I make a point of saying 'every name possible'. In his *Notebook of a Return to My Native Land* ([1938]1995), Aimé Césaire

2 Simone Schwarz-Bart, *Between Two Worlds* (Barbara Bray trans.) (New York: Harper and Row, 1981).

laments: 'I am of no nationality provided for by the chan-celleries.'[3] Today this lament is laughable. Nationality! We now know how meaningless this term is. We have already been taught it by the colonial 'mother countries' imposing on our peoples borrowed nationalities. We now know that its only purpose is, in fact, to obtain green, blue, red or orange biometric passports, depending on the country, that allow the holders to cross borders and work in peace in a given place. Caribbean people while away their days under American, Canadian, German and Spanish nationalities. What does it matter provided writers and artists are allowed to keep their creativity intact? Hearts and creative thoughts attach little importance to the lines at Immigration. They settle everywhere and flourish anywhere they please. For them, continents drift and majestic tropical forests can thrive in the very middle of a sidewalk in Manhattan.

So here is the Caribbean with no fixed abode. It is not necessarily regrettable, may we say again. Strangled by their cramped, overpopulated islands, the peoples of the Caribbean are suddenly offered the vast world and its wide expanses open to the heart. As a result their egos swell and they are elated.

It would be interesting to compare texts by the 'Caribbean Insider' and those neo-Caribbean nomads. Which of them has the greatest freedom of expression? Which text has the most luxuriant descriptions? In short, what are the differences between reality and the imagined?

What does the Caribbean nomad (creator or not, that is not the question) have left to define himself?

---

3 Aimé Césaire, *Notebook of a Return to My Native Land*, bilingual edn (Mireille Rosello, with Annie Pritchard trans) (Northumberland, UK: Bloodaxe Books, 1995), p. 107.

His language? But which one? The language of the colonizer or his native tongue?

Here we touch upon a prickly question.

At the end of the fifteenth century, when Christopher Columbus reached the Antilles and presented its lands to Spain, Antonio de Nebrija, Bishop of Avila, advised Queen Isabella of Spain that 'language is the perfect instrument of empire.'

Every colonizing nation has shared this point of view. The Jamaicans, Trinidadians and Barbadians were commanded to use English and to go into raptures over daffodils they had heard mentioned only in the poem by William Wordsworth. Across the Caribbean basin, the so-called high-civilization languages of Europe imposed an aura of silence. At home in Guadeloupe and Martinique, French sent Creole packing at the school gates and then banished it completely. For the entire Caribbean, the European or colonial language became much more than a symbol of education—it became the supreme fetish before which everyone bowed low. Frantz Fanon in *Black Skin, White Masks* ([1952] 2008) ironically describes the love relationship between the black man and the French language.[4] In every island, except during episodic movements of revolt, the native tongue is marginalized. Within the immigrant community, after one or two generations at most it disappears. One of the main criticisms voiced by the Guadeloupeans against the Negropolitans coming from France on holiday is the latter's inability to speak Creole.

Oddly enough, in my opinion, the Caribbean writer has always escaped this pure and simple subjection to the

4 See Frantz Fanon, *Black Skin, White Masks* (Richard Philcox trans.) (New York: Grove Press, 2008).

colonial language because he knows he has to coin his own idiom. He has no native tongue. Every language is foreign to him, even hostile. Mauritian poet Édouard Maunick somewhat crudely summed up this urgency located at the heart of literary creation when he declared: 'The French language is a beautiful woman. I have sex with her and give her bastards.'[5]

The Martinican Creolists wrongly believe themselves to be the first and only ones to have liberated themselves from the French language. Césaire (yes, Césaire himself, whatever Raphaël Confiant thinks!) endeavoured to do the same, resorting to words borrowed from Latin and Greek, unusual and rarely used terms, such as 'eschare', 'impaludé', 'hypoglosse' and 'pérégrine' (to quote haphazardly from the first pages of Césaire's *Notebook*) and all kinds of neologisms, such as Negritude, lest we forget.

> My negritude is not a stone, its deafness hurled
> against the clamour of the day
>
> My negritude is not an opaque spot of dead water
> over the dead eye of the earth.[6]

The originality of the Creolists lies precisely in the way they make use of the silenced tongue, as Jacques Coursil named it,[7] the tongue that was never allowed to speak in order to subvert the French literary space.

In *Solibo Magnificent* ([1988] 1998), Patrick Chamoiseau writes:

5 At a conference on La Francophone, Université Paris Nord, 1972.

6 Césaire, *Notebook*, p. 115.

7 See Jacques Coursil, 'Eloge de la Muette' in *La fonction muette du langage: Essai de linguistique générale contemporaine* (Petit-Bourg, Guadeloupe: Ibis Rouge, 2000), pp. 149–66.

> Congo told him of a strangulation of the speech and Bouaffesse remained silent, suspicious, wondering if he had heard correctly. He stammered out for an explanation: 'Papa, I don't understand how speech can strangle someone?'
>
> 'Ha di yo di'w!' Congo admitted.
>
> Which in another language can mean: 'Neither do I!'[8]

Here, however, we are dealing with three 'writers on the inside' (Césaire, Chamoiseau and Confiant) who, rooted to their native soil, left their island for no more than brief sojourns. What about the others, all the others, who were born and carried to where the wind of survival took their parents? We should note from the outset that the gap between 'writers on the inside' and 'writers on the outside' (increasingly numerous, dynamic and appreciated in their country of adoption) is widening and that perhaps it is time to close it. In the USA, these 'outside writers' are called hyphenated writers—Cuban-Americans, Haitian-Americans. In a country where everyone respects, at least orally, the other's origins, this comes down to considering them fully fledged citizens. Their situations vary. Let us quickly cite a few examples: Esmeralda Santiago, from Puerto Rico, author of the revealingly titled novel *When I Was Puerto Rican* (1993);[9] Cristina García and Julia Alvarez, both from Cuba, authors forsaking the Spanish for English. In all three cases, the novels are of a classic and entertaining construction and the descriptions of their adaptation to a new society are seasoned with a touch of nostalgia for the

8 Patrick Chamoiseau, *Solibo Magnificent* (Rose-Myriam Réjouis and Val Vinokurov trans) (New York: Alfred A. Knopf, 1998), p. 65.

9 Esmerelda Santiago, *When I Was Puerto Rican* (New York: Da Capo Press, 2006).

old. There is no evident stylistic extravagance in their switch to English except for a few phrases in Spanish, here and there. Edwidge Danticat and Myriam Chancy, both from Haiti, do likewise, turning their back on French to write in English. Even though they use an identical medium, their work is very different: Chancy's books are instilled with feminism and introspection; her language is poetic, even erudite, whereas Danticat's is simpler, clearer and slightly mundane. One important factor is the frequent use of Creole, especially in her last book *Brother, I'm Dying* (2007), that is absent in Chancy's work.[10] Between the words in English, the Creole rears up like a stubborn and rebellious memory. A memory that refuses to die. In the words of Jean Metellus, to compensate for the physical separation, Creole links Danticat to a 'pathetic', suffering island.[11] This is evident when reviewing the topics of her novels: the exodus of boat people, the massacre of Haitian cane cutters in the Dominican Republic, the presence of a former Tonton Macoute in a house in Brooklyn, her father's death and her uncle's imprisonment. We can easily see that this Second Generation, in spite of its sociological jargon, keeps very close to traditional Caribbean models. Despite the distance that separates them, Danticat follows Césaire, in her own way:

> My mouth will be the mouth of those griefs which have no mouth, my voice, the freedom of those that collapse in the dungeon of despair.[12]

10 Edwidge Danticat, *Brother, I'm Dying* (New York: Alfred A. Knopf, 2007).

11 During a dialogue with Caribbean writers at Bibliothèque Nationale de Paris, October 1998.

12 Césaire, *Notebook*, p. 89.

Despite changes in narration and technique (which we won't go into here), Danticat has kept practically intact the sense of the literary function by the writers on the inside. We cannot put in doubt her 'Caribbeanness'. Or should we say 'Caribbeanitude'? Let us see whether her future works describe to us the anguish of her dilemma. For the time being, except for the linguistic shift which by no means appears as a transgression, this writer's heart and imagination, unlike Chancy's, have not radically discovered the Other Place.

The most complex case is undoubtedly that of Junot Díaz, from Santo Domingo. In the USA, Díaz is a phenomenon, greeted as a genius by critics throughout the country. For weeks, his novel *The Brief Wondrous Life of Oscar Wao* (2007) rode high on the best-seller lists.[13] Taking as a pretext the story of a Dominican family exiled to New Jersey, Díaz attacks the dictatorship of Trujillo, a subject dealt with more traditionally by Mario Vargas Llosa in *The Feast of the Goat* (2000).[14] Díaz does a makeover of the topic and gives us a new version of history and intertwining stories. He mercilessly drags us in pursuit of a raving mad narrator who is split between hatred and compassion. He describes to us a gallery of obscene portraits that are, nevertheless, surprisingly familiar. The most spectacular aspect of the novel is its style—he shamelessly juxtaposes both an unconventional English and Spanish. But this runs the risk of seeming incomprehensible or tiresome to the reader. Especially those who, like me, cannot read Spanish and must arm

13 Junot Díaz, *The Brief Wondrous Life of Oscar Wao* (New York: Riverhead Books, 2007).

14 Mario Vargas Llosa, *The Feast of the Goat* (Edith Grossman trans.) (New York: Farrar, Straus and Giroux, 2000).

themselves with a dictionary or wait for a French translation. The juxtaposition of two languages in a text is nothing new, and was initiated many years ago by Chicana writer Gloria Anzaldúa in *Borderlands / La Frontera: The New Mestiza* (1987). She aimed at translating the complexity of a culture where the values of Mexican immigrants collide with those of the Americans in Southern California, renamed Aztlán, while she the writer is caught in the middle. 'In such a case,' she writes, 'hatred, anger and exploitation are unavoidable.'[15] Fortunately, according to her, the situation is but temporary and precedes the time of a joint transformation, a 'Creolization' considered more peaceful. As for Díaz, he offers no vision of the future. When will this Creolization that Anzaldúa dreams of occur? What shape will it take? Will a new being emerge? What will he look like? What language will he speak?

In conclusion, what can we say of this all too succinct presentation of the Caribbean and its literature at the start of this twenty-first century? For many of its writers, the old values are shifting. Place of residence, nationality and even language are all being relativized and redefined. Everything is possible. Everything is to be born. Everything is to be named or renamed. Isn't this inevitable in this changing world undergoing massive transformation? The mistake consists in preserving erroneous categories and using definitions that no longer correspond to anything meaningful.

15 See 'Preface' in Gloria Anzaldúa, *Borderlands / La Frontera: The New Mestiza* (San Francisco: Aunt Lute, 1987), n.p.

Instructions on How to Become a 'Caribbean' Writer

If I want to clarify the origins of my literary career I have to go back when I was nine or ten, to an episode that occurred on my mother's birthday. I have already described it in my childhood memoirs *Tales from the Heart* ([1998] 2001) and the reason I am reliving it today is because it had enormous consequences.[1] We are constantly called upon to answer that bombshell of a question: 'When did you decide to become a writer?' as if the decision to opt for an unrewarding, underpaid activity loaded with pitfalls and perils was resolved with the wave of a wand. Without over-embellishing reality I can now safely say that my vocation was born on that day in some year on 28 April.

My family prided itself on being picture perfect in public. On Sundays at High Mass, when my brothers, sisters and I knelt in a row with my mother—as a freethinker, my father, like all men of his rank, did not attend church—we were supposed to be a family manifesting perfect harmony and faith in God. My mother's birthday corresponded to

Originally published as 'Mode d'emploi. Comment devenir une écrivaine que l'on dit antillaise', *Nouvelles Etudes Francophones* 22(1) (Spring 2007): 47–51.

1 Maryse Condé, *Tales from the Heart: True Stories from My Childhood* (Richard Philcox trans.) (New York: Soho Press, 2001).

this obsession with setting an example. Besides her children, she would invite her best pupils from class and a few carefully selected friends. To the tinkle of champagne coupes for the adults, glasses of barley water for the younger ones and coconut sorbet for everyone, some would perform a short play, others recite poems. The more gifted guests would play compositions on the piano or the violin, sometimes the flute. At the end, my father would present my mother with a piece of jewellery that was then handed round so that those who had their doubts could check its weight. I suppose on that particular year I did not want to be content with playing the pathetic role of the youngest as usual. I announced to everyone that I was preparing a short play. Or was it a dramatic poem? In verse or in prose? I no longer recall the form of this first work nor the source of my inspiration. All I remember was that I worked tirelessly on it in the greatest of secrecy. My creation revolved round a sole character—my mother, whom I adored but whose complex nature had some disconcerting facets. How could the same person smother me with kisses one moment and give me such a violent cuff the next? Call me 'my treasure, my *doudou*', then publicly humiliate me?

When my turn came that day, I paraded in front of her for a good forty-five minutes. The stony silence should have warned me. When I finally stopped, waiting for the applause that was a long time coming, my mother, who had listened to me without flinching, her eyes glistening with tears, murmured: 'So that's how you see me?'

The feeling of power I felt that afternoon at making my mother cry, I, a child no taller than a tuft of Guinea grass, as thin as a mosquito, I have sought the same feeling book after book. Oh, to take people down a peg! Burst the abscess! Denounce the hordes of hypocrites, religious

nutcases and do-gooders! Trample on the *idées reçues* and
the lies! Shout loud and clear that the emperor, wherever
his crown comes from, has no clothes! When Edmond
Jabès declares that there is no writing without lies, he is
mistaken.[2] There is no writing worthy of the name without the concern for truth. Didn't Césaire give the most
striking example when he dared to describe the isles,
crowned   paradises by generations of men of letters?

> At the brink of dawn, budding with frail creeks,
> the hungry West Indies, the West Indies pockpit-
> ted with smallpox, the West Indies blown up by
> alcohol, stranded in the mud of this bay, in the
> dust of this town sordidly stranded.[3]

This is why, from my very first novel *Heremakhonon*
([1976] 1982), I took on one of the most sacred of myths.[4]
For political and sentimental reasons that would take too
long to explain here, I was living in the Guinea of Sékou
Touré who, a few years earlier, had proudly carved a reputation for himself by saying 'No' to General de Gaulle. A
lot had happened since. His dictatorship slowly settled into
place. The infamous Boiro Camp had not yet opened its
cells but thousands were already fleeing into exile. Where
then was the revolution? I couldn't see it anywhere. Above
the sorry roofs of the shacks my eyes could see only
the silent, suffering, ill-nourished masses, students imprisoned, patriots assassinated and arrogant bourgeois driving
round the heaps of garbage in their Mercedes Benzes.
Deep down, I was quite pleased with my first attempt. In

2 Edmond Jabès, *Le livre des questions*, I (Paris: Gallimard, 1963).

3 Césaire, *Notebook*, p. 73.

4 Maryse Condé, *Heremakhonon* (Richard Philcox trans.) (Washington, DC: Three Continents Press, 1982).

order to make my argument more powerful, I believed I had created one of the most plausible anti-heroines. So as to convey her alienation and interior confusion, I had eliminated any verbal statements on her part. As a result, all dialogue had disappeared; I left it to the reader to reconstruct her thoughts and words. To my surprise, all these literary subtleties were swept away and ignored. I had not drawn all the lessons from my mother's tears. I had not realized that there is a heavy price to pay for the truth which offends and hurts—the heavy price of unpopularity and denigration. No sooner was my first book off the press than I numbered among the most unpopular writers of the Negro-African world. (Is this adjective still in use? Shouldn't it be shelved with so many others, such as socialism, Marxism, Pan-Africanism, even idealism?)

I was accused of not 'loving' Africa, a reproach that hurt me, especially as it was totally unjustified. I dressed my wounds as best I could and endeavoured to cast out the nines to prove my feelings. I launched into writing *Segu: Murailles de terre* ([1984] 1987), the saga of a thousand pages where I symbolically claimed my Bambara ancestor.[5] At the same time, I intended to demonstrate how my literary work had evolved. No more Michel Leiris or even Philip Roth whose *Portnoy's Complaint* (1969)[6] had filled me with an envy that left me powerless. How could I ever manage to write a book like that? My role models were no longer these French or American writers. It was the griots, their

5 Maryse Condé, *Segu* (Barbara Bray trans.) (New York: Viking, 1987). *Ségou: La Terre en miettes,* part 2 of this African saga, was published in 1985 and is available in English as: *The Children of Segu* (Linda Coverdale trans.) (New York: Penguin, 1989).

6 Philip Roth, *Portnoy's Complaint* (New York: Random House, 1969).

talking drums under their arms, whose paths I had crossed in Guinea and those in Mali who were the true masters of the art of storytelling. In order to claim their filiation, I proudly began with an anonymous epigraph on the region of the Joliba I so admired: 'Segu is a garden where cunning grows. Segu is built on treachery. Speak of Segu outside Segu, but do not speak of Segu in Segu.'[7]

Alas! Once again literary considerations counted little when the book was published. The critics and uncompromising African readers retained only the depiction of Islam from the medley of stories. Always my wretched concern for the truth! I had unwisely been inspired by information provided by my sources that told me that the Bambara, commonly despised as 'fetishists' or 'animists', had the bad idea of cherishing their ancestral gods who inhabited and animated the immensity of nature. In fact, the monotheistic religion had to be forced upon them by a bloody jihad led by the Toucouleurs of El Hadj Omar Saidou Tall, who had long ago converted to Islam. My sources even made the unfortunate decision to take me to the mass graves where the Bambara 'infidels', duly massacred, had been buried pell-mell. To the previous criticisms was added that of a freethinker, dangerous and sacrilegious. Matters came to such a point that I decided to leave a mother who in the end turned out to be a cruel stepmother.

I gathered up my meagre possessions and my numerous children and returned home. But not anyone can write *Notebook of a Return to My Native Land*. The Guadeloupe I landed on was virtually terra incognita.

The circumstances of my education had undermined a certain form of intimacy between the island and me. I

7 Condé, *Segu*, p. 3.

remembered only some of its superficial physical features. For example, I knew its shores were fringed with a thick blue line, that some days the rain fell tirelessly and monotonously and at night the frogs and giant toads tried in vain to rival the crazed voice of the wind. The local intellectuals saw it. They stared at me. Why hadn't I stayed where I was! Was I really a Guadeloupean? They could tell by looking at me that I had not grown up with the tales of Zamba and Rabbit. Had I ever attended a *léwoz* dance? Or an ox pull? Did I like the *mazouk* or the *gwoka* music? They kept the sharpest barb for the last: Did I know how to speak Creole, the language of the emotions forged in the horrors of the plantation system? Was I planning to use this magnificent and unrecognized resource in my writing? Let there be no mistake—I fought back tooth and nail. Despite appearances, I had read all of Fanon. When I was living in Guinea, three days of national mourning was declared on his death and the town's main thoroughfare renamed after him. Some are content to settle for that while awaiting the coming of the revolution. Tales of Zamba and Rabbit? Ox pulls? *Mazouk*? *Gwoka*? Did my critics want to reduce Antillean culture to these worn-out clichés? Did they want me to quote *The Wretched of the Earth* for them? 'The culture with which the intellectual is preoccupied is very often nothing but an inventory of particularisms. Seeking to cling close to the people, he clings merely to a visible veneer. This veneer, however, is merely a reflection of a dense subterranean life in perpetual renewal.'[8]

As for Creole, it's a fact I don't speak it well enough to consider using it in my writing. But what does it matter?

8 Frantz Fanon, *The Wretched of the Earth* (Richard Philcox trans.) (New York: Grove Press, 2005), p. 160.

Do we have to confine ourselves over and over again to the Weberian definitions of another age, such as French / colonial language versus Creole / mother tongue? I called to the rescue Roland Barthes, Julia Kristeva and, above all, Mikhail Bakhtin invoking heteroglossia, hybridity of language and its powers of double voice. Even Marcel Proust was made to contribute. Hadn't he written in *Contre Sainte-Beuve*: 'Great literature is written in a sort of foreign tongue'?[9]

Needless to say, no one heard me and I didn't have the last word.

Once again, I decided to leave an island which was native only in name. As you will have seen, changes of scenery and what they call nomadism do not frighten me.

I know what you are thinking. You are wondering how this farrago of a story ends? It doesn't. Well, not yet, but it will do, for all things come to an end as everyone knows. In the place where I have chosen to live I am protected by my foreignness. I have nothing in common with those round me: neither language, nor history, stories, food, nursery rhymes nor other childhood memories. I write my novels, then, with a peace of mind whenever I please. It does so happen that some of them are translated into the local idiom. But these are translations and therefore for me totally foreign. Translation has always seemed to me the final stage of this dispossession of one's text; it begins with the fight to keep one's title, the arbitrary choice of an usually terrible cover and ends with the writing of a catchy blurb for the back cover. The reception in a language other

9 Marcel Proust, *Contre Sainte-Beuve*, 'The Return to the Present' in *On Art and Literature: 1896–1919* (Sylvia Townsend Warner trans.) (New York: Caroll and Graf, 1984), pp. 265–78; here, p. 267.

than the one I have endeavoured to create to the best of my ability is of little concern to me. Yet I still meet with misadventures from time to time. For example, when I presented my novel *The Story of the Cannibal Woman* ([2005] 2007) at a book party organized by some friends, no one was interested in my attempts (that I thought commendable) to introduce a polyphonic narrative voice.[10] Who is speaking in this novel? Is it Rosélie, the main character? Is it the narrator? Is it the author? The South African ambassador who was attending the party criticized fairly strongly my depiction of her country. How was I to defend myself? Was it my fault that I wept at the memory of Nelson Mandela's trials and tribulations when I visited Robben Island, now transformed into an international tourist attraction? If the hideous belt of shanty towns round Cape Town, so luxurious and so white, made me feel sick?

I sometimes tell myself that the solution would be to stop travelling, to stay at home, to no longer open doors and windows and to live and write in seclusion.

Alas! It's impossible! The world is out there calling me and won't leave me in peace.

Columbia University

---

10 Maryse Condé, *The Story of the Cannibal Woman* (Richard Philcox trans.) (New York: Simon and Schuster, 2007).

Intimate Enemies

A WRITER'S REFLECTION ON TRANSLATION

A few years back I was invited by the Columbia University's Institute for Comparative Literature and Society under the direction of Professor Gayatri Chakravorty Spivak to have a conversation with Richard Philcox on the subject of translation. For over thirty years, Richard Philcox, also my husband, has been translating my books into English. The idea behind the conversation was to clarify what everyone thought was a close collaboration and a joint effort.

My first reaction was to refuse the invitation. I know nothing of the problems relating to the art of translation. I do know that, during the Renaissance, translations of popular Latin and Greek texts were jokingly referred to as 'the unfaithful lovelies'. I was also familiar with the famous Italian reproach, now a proverb: 'Traduttore traditore'.

On more serious matters: I had read a good many books on the subject of translation, from the seminal work *After Babel* by George Steiner (1975)[1] and articles by Walter Benjamin to essays by Yves Bonnefoy, Antoine Berman, Susan Bassnett and Maurice Blanchot.

Written in 2010. Unpublished.

1 George Steiner, *After Babel* (London: Oxford University Press, 1975).

But above all, with Richard, I had listened to many a lecture and attended numerous workshops where translators discussed their work. I had been especially impressed by John Felstiner discussing his translations of Pablo Neruda and Paul Celan. I had also met many translators. Although very different from one another, like Edith Grossman who did a fresh translation of *Don Quixote* that was hailed unanimously by the press, to Alyson Waters, professor at Yale University, an advocate for publishing non-canonical foreign authors so as to expand the American literary horizon, they all had one thing in common— an extreme sensitivity, bordering sometimes on aggression.

Translation, however, is not only disparaged by the disgruntled, some of whom go as far as saying that it is quite simply an impossible task. The relationship between authors and their translators is often complex, even tainted with negative comments. Poet Robert Frost, for instance, cruelly stated that poetry is what gets lost in translation unlike Kazuo Ishiguro who urged his peers, the English novelists, to simplify their writing in order to help their translators; and we all know Milan Kundera's position on the subject—he is convinced that translation distorts and flattens his style. In his essay *Testaments Betrayed* ([1993] 1995), Kundera takes umbrage with translators who are primarily obsessed with the problem of 'correcting' the language and not with respecting the linguistic originality of the author whose works they are making available in another tongue.[2]

I thought that I had no personal views on the subject. Contrary to common belief, there is no collaboration

2 See Milan Kundera, *Testaments Betrayed: An Essay in Nine Parts* (Linda Asher trans.) (New York: HarperCollins, 1995).

between Richard and me. We work separately, practically in autarchy. Given the difficulties he has in interesting American editors in a book written in French by a Guadeloupean writer, any novel he translates is at least two or three years old and has long been published in France. Once it is published, I never read his translation on the pretext that the foreign versions of my books are no concern of mine. Richard does not seem to be surprised or to take offence at such an attitude. On the contrary, he is only too happy, saying that it gives him total freedom in his work. It also gives him the opportunity to elaborate his theory on the fidelity or infidelity of the translator (as he has done at numerous conferences, even as far away as Australia in 2005).

The invitation by the Institute for Comparative Literature and Society encouraged me to embark upon a new introspection of myself. I am an author who is fairly widely translated and, as a result, constantly approached by Dutch, Polish or Italian translators. Unlike Richard, who has lived with me for many years in the Antilles, they have seldom travelled to Guadeloupe and know practically nothing of its flora or culture. I answer their questions, often naive in my opinion, as best I can. But I have no way of guaranteeing their comprehension and even less of assessing the quality of their final translation. Not only am I incapable of reading or judging it but all I have are a few unusable author's copies sent by the editor which I put away in a drawer after a mere glance. For the first time I asked myself an important question. Refusing to read the English translations by Richard came down to treating in the same way not only the versions published in a foreign language but also the works of my own translator in a language I know full well. Wasn't that odd? What lay behind such an illogical reaction?

In one of my recent books, devoted to my grandmother who was a peerless cook, I write:

> Victoire did not appreciate the fuss made of her person. She reluctantly confided in Anne-Marie the secret of her culinary compositions so that the latter could name them and have them printed. As with a writer whose editor decides the title, cover and illustrations of her book, it was partly like being dispossessed of her creation. She would have preferred to keep it secret. For her, cooking in no way implied wreaking vengeance on a society that had never made room for her. More than music, where she never excelled at playing the guitar or the flute, it was her way of expressing herself, which was constantly repressed, prisoner of her illiteracy, her illegitimacy, her gender and her station as a servant. When she invented seasoning or blended flavors, her personality was set free and blossomed. Cooking was her Père Labat rum, her ganja, her crack, her ecstasy. She dominated the world. For a time she became God. Once again, like a writer.[3]

The comparison of the writer to God is nothing new. But we forget all too often how jealous God is, although the Bible never stops reminding us.

The relationship between an author and her text can be compared to no other. It is closer than the ties between a mother and her children who, no sooner than the umbilical cord is cut, manifest a regrettable tendency to break free. A text can never break free. It is an absolute creation.

3 Maryse Condé, *Victoire, My Mother's Mother* (Richard Philcox trans.) (New York: Simon and Schuster, 2010), p. 71.

We would be mistaken, in fact, to believe literally those novelists who love to claim that their characters have a mind of their own. It is merely an image. A book's characters, in fact, are constantly under close surveillance and the novelist keeps strict control over their freedom.

A writer may seem a peculiar being. Even if the weather outside is lovely he spends hours and hours locked up in his room. What does he do there? He builds sentences, pores over words, even punctuation. He toys with them, rejecting some and retaining others. He means to be as close as possible to the mysterious voice that haunts him and which he alone can hear. So as to remain porous to its slightest inflexion, some writers resort to various stimulants. Personally, I resort to the music of certain musicians who open, then irrigate, the valves of my creativity while instilling a precious spirit of competition. Other writers, on the contrary, require total silence. In this apparently fastidious task the writer finds his happiness. He gets a kick. Out of his omnipotence.

Paradoxically, once all these endeavours have been brought to a conclusion, the book finished and slated for publication, everything begins to get complicated. This is when the writer emerges from his happy/harrowing retreat and confronts an individual—his editor. Far be it from me to suggest that editors and authors do not agree. Nothing would be farther from the truth. Authors and editors complement each other, united for better or for worse by the success or failure of a book that involves them both. Nevertheless, they have different, even opposite, concerns. The editor is obliged to sell an object that today has lost a lot of its appeal and is consequently governed by commercial considerations. Once the book has been launched, his greatest terror is a stream of returns from booksellers. His crowning joy would be one or two reprints.

As for the writer, she is increasingly riddled with doubt about the quality of her work and wonders whether her voice will manage to be heard and, even more importantly, appeal to readers during the commotion of the literary season. As a result, it is unavoidable that author and editor do not always see eye to eye. There are all sorts of objects of contention. In the case of a Caribbean writer, they include the decision to add a glossary at the end of the book and footnotes explaining Creole words and expressions. The author is usually against it whereas the editor, little convinced by the 'theory of opacity', considers it indispensable for understanding the book. Then comes the problem of the cover. Except for the rare exception, the art seldom matches my text. I can remember the endless debates over the cover for *Segu*. It had to be simple, clear and accessible to all. Then comes the problem of the blurb on the back cover. To be fair, the editor often asks the author to write it himself but he seldom keeps to what is proposed. Few realize that the back cover is the result of painstaking adjustments and endless compromise.

The main object of discord, however, remains the title on which major issue the author does not always have the last word. In my case, I could mention many a battle I have waged; I recently lost one when I had to give up the title I had chosen, *Les pareurs de mort* (The Dressers of Death), and replace it with *Les belles ténébreuses* (The Brooding Beauties).[4]

4 Maryse Condé, *Les belles ténébreuses* (Paris: Mercure de France, 2008). Yet to be translated.

As the hour of publication gradually approaches, the writer feels increasingly feverish, anxious and ill at ease. Gone is the feeling of omnipotence and the marvellous freedom he enjoyed. He sees enemies everywhere. In the shape of journalists he is about to meet. Even if they are not entirely malicious, they will only have flipped through his book superficially. The writer dreads above all the readers who read only what they want to. Let us not forget Simone de Beauvoir's cruel point of view—that a writer should never meet her readers.

If the editor of the original book is delighted to have found a translation, it is not purely for commercial reasons. It benefits everyone. By widening the author's readership and guaranteeing access to his work to readers across the world, it offers him the possibility of an extended life and promises him—who knows?—immortality. Edith Grossman writes affirmatively in *Why Translation Matters* (2010) that, without a translation into English, no author can earn a living.[5] For us writers from Guadeloupe, Martinique and French Guiana, we hear over and over again that a translation is not only a blessing but almost a political success. Thanks to translation, our tiny, insignificant and unheard-of islands will emerge from the shadows and take their place on the map. The writer thus sees himself crowned not only spokesman but also ambassador for his region.

I have never believed in such myths. Especially because the majority of Guadeloupeans have never endorsed the way my novels depict our island. On the contrary, I have been the object of sharp criticism. Writers, moreover, who do not go along with these myths represent a minority.

5 See Edith Grossman, *Why Translation Matters* (New Haven, CT: Yale University Press, 2010).

They know that they are a threat to the freedom of the majority. For many of us, matters are secretly lived very differently from these clichés. The appropriation of our texts by others and their transformation without our control are seen as illegitimate acts. For me and many other authors who dare not admit it, a translation is seen as the ultimate stage of dispossession that begins as soon as its publication is announced.

In order to fully understand this feeling, let us recall once again the circumstances surrounding literary creation. For weeks, months, even years (time is of no importance), the book has been distilled into the author's ear, word by word, metaphor by metaphor and punctuation mark by punctuation mark in close intimacy. Don't ask how. Previously, there was talk of inspiration. Now the term is no longer applicable and creation remains a great mystery.

During a certain time, then, the author is alone with his obsessions, his fantasies and his fears which have woven the fabric of his text. He is responsible for every meander of every sentence. What makes the author's reaction even more complex is that words do not simply have a meaning. Like musical notes, they have a sound. Placed end to end they not only compose a meaningful story but also music: sonata, symphony or concerto. Without possessing the genius of Mozart or Dvořák, every writer, nevertheless, produces a similar work. He composes a score. We all recall Gustave Flaubert's example of declaiming his texts aloud, his 'gueuloir', to check their oral harmony.[6]

So what is the task of the translator?

6 See, for example, Pierre-Marc de Biasi, 'Flaubert: le travail de l'écriture' in Anne-Marie Christin (ed.), *Histoire de l'écriture. De l'idéogramme au multimédia* (Paris: Flammarion, 2001), pp. 340–1. A discussion of

It consists of using words belonging to another idiom, in other words, his, i.e. words different from those chosen by the author after a long selection process. The translator turns the musicality of the text upside down and in the end destroys the lovingly elaborated score. In the course of this annihilation, the author's voice disappears and he is excluded from the text he so patiently produced. What voice then prevails and replaces the author's? It can only be that of the translator! He is responsible not only for the choice of new words but also their arrangement and their dance of seduction, for words make love if we are to believe André Breton. And, above all, don't think you can reassure the author by reminding him that the translator will not modify the essentials, i.e. the meaning of his text. He knows it is not exactly true. Every language has its own system, its own way of saying things. Here again the author feels betrayed.

Appropriation. Treason. Exclusion.

These are apparently serious accusations. But not for the author. He is close to seeing the translator as the most formidable enemy he has ever crossed paths with, more formidable than the journalists, readers and editors.

After having confronted these truths for the first time, I felt liberated. I realized that in my case the problem resided not so much with the translations in the language I did not understand but precisely with the one I did. Here I can judge the translator's work, i.e. assess the extent of the transformation compared to the original text. By refusing to read them and placing the translations in

Flaubert's writing process, based on this and other works, may be found at www.onfiction.ca/2009/02/art-of-prose-fiction-i-flaubert. html (last accessed 1 August 2013).

Hebrew, Serbo-Croat, Korean or English on the same level, I was endeavouring to protect myself and preserve my inalienable rights as a creator.

Finally, I accepted the Institute's invitation. For the first time, I expressed my personal point of view on translation. I don't know how my thoughts were received. With surprise, I imagine. What I do know is that while I was speaking I was aware of both a paradox and the feeling of a monstrous hypocrisy.

I live in the USA where my books are published and read in English. They are taught in American universities and reviewed by American researchers and students. I had just been awarded the Hurston-Wright Legacy Award for a novel that goes under the name of *Who Slashed Celanire's Throat?* (2004) American readers are unaware of the original title—*Celanire Cou-Coupé* (2000)—whose literary references to Apollinaire and Césaire apparently went unnoticed and had very little impact.[7] I climbed onto the stage to accept the prize and thanked the jury but I did not take the opportunity to express my lack of interest in the English translation and state that it was none of my business. Why hadn't I invited Richard to receive this award instead of leaving him in the crowd of spectators?

As translator Tim Parks writes: 'The translator should do his job and then disappear. The great, charismatic creative writer wants to be all over the globe. And the last thing he wants to accept is that the majority of his readers are not really reading him.'[8]

7 Maryse Condé, *Who Slashed Celanire's Throat? A Fantastical Tale* (Richard Philcox trans.) (New York: Simon and Schuster, 2004).

8 Tim Parks, 'Why Translators Deserve Some Credit', *The Observer*, 25 April 2010, p. 43.

I had never realized how thankless the job of the translator really is. His name is relegated to the third or fourth page of the book, seldom next to the author's. Some publishing houses omit it altogether, although this is increasingly rare. The press barely mentions the quality of his work. These issues, however, which appear to be wounds of self-esteem, are not the most serious. Grossman exposes the major hurdle a translator must overcome: 'It is fascinating and puzzling to realize that only translation has to fend off the insidious, damaging question of whether or not it is, can be, or should be possible. It would never occur to anyone to ask whether it is feasible for an actor to perform a dramatic role or a musician to interpret a piece of music.'[9]

The topic is open to debate. Is translation possible?

It is a well-known fact that every language implies a culture, in other words, it conveys a specific history, a sum of given experiences. This is why some people regularly condemn the linguistic dimension of colonialism. The colonized subject who uses the language of the colonizer is said to wear a borrowed coat and to travesty the expression of his inner self. If we admit this theory, then it is impossible to transpose a work from one language into another. In doing so, we run the danger of irremediably deflowering the specificity of a text and its unique and singular nature.

My introspection went deeper and considered these objections from every angle. They weren't mine. Lest we forget, it is through translations that we read the masterpieces of universal literature. I am not just speaking of the

9 Grossman, *Why Translation Matters*, p. 12.

Greek and Roman classics but also of the works by Dante Alighieri, Miguel de Cervantes, Fyodor Dostoevsky, Italo Calvino, Yasunari Kawabata and Orhan Pamuk. Paradoxically, translation has given me great joy. Some of my best memories are of Tokyo where I was surrounded by Japanese readers unable to read me in the original. With its limits, translation appears to me to be a necessary evil. My reservations towards it are merely a product of my narcissism and is the jealousy of an author who dreads being dispossessed and who thus sees enemies everywhere. If the translator has to be counted among the enemies, he is a particular species of enemy, as indispensable and as intimate as a friend. All things considered, I ran the risk of seeming to side with the detractors and proving their criticisms right. I had to clarify my position as quickly as possible. Soon, however, I was besieged with other considerations.

Octavio Paz wrote in 'Translation, Literature and Letters' (1971) the magnificent phrase: 'When we are learning to speak we are learning to translate.'[10] He goes on to explain that children translate the unknown round them in a language which gradually becomes familiar to them; that we are constantly engaged in a thought process. So we are all translators. These reflections touch the very core of creation.

It is extremely difficult to pinpoint the moment when a literary vocation is born. In my case, I can think of a series of moments that awoke in me the confused idea of becoming a writer. In my childhood memoirs I describe

10 Octavio Paz, 'Translation, Literature and Letters' in Rainer Schulte and John Biguenet (eds), *Theories of Translation: An Anthology of Essays from Dryden to Derrida* (Chicago: University of Chicago Press, 1992), pp. 152–62; here, p. 152.

one of them—the one that happened on my mother's birthday. Here is another which is perhaps even more important.

I was ten or twelve at the most. My parents owned a 'change of air house', as they were called, in a place named Sarcelles, Petit-Bourg (nothing to do with the suburb of Paris with the same name). Open fields stretched as far as the eye could see, tall grass, scrub, guava and jujube trees grew freely, squeezed between the ocean and the chain of mountains topped by the wisps of smoke from the Soufrière volcano. It wasn't a region that was particularly liked by the Guadeloupeans—it was too flat and the black sand in mourning of the beach at Viard was sometimes muddy. The two neighbouring towns of Petit-Bourg and Goyave were merely conglomerations of indistinguishable shacks. Yet if you opened your heart to it, it answered in no uncertain way.

One day, with a band of children my age, I went looking for coco plums—those little white, pink or black berries with a lightly perfumed and soft flesh that have now completely disappeared from our countryside. They used to be every child's delight. Just as I was about to grab my prey I was overcome by an extraordinary emotion caused by the grassy ocean rippling as far as the eye could see, the massive contours of the mountains, the blue strip of the sea on the horizon and, above all that, the sun pouring down its golden rays in abundance. I stood still, endeavouring to drink in every detail of the sight. Oddly enough, I felt like crying and at the same time shouting and stamping my feet.

'What's the matter?' one of my friends asked.

Without answering I turned and ran back as fast as I could to the house. I rushed in and locked myself in my room. I grabbed a pen, a notepad and attempted to 'translate' (I use the word on purpose) what I was feeling. Unfortunately, this composition has long disappeared. I know only it was followed by many others. I kept the green-cover exercise book, where I hid my first attempts at writing, for a long time. So as to elude my mother who had the annoying habit of checking my desk for forbidden books, I wrote 'Rough Drafts' on the cover.

Dangerous Liaison

I am very fond of saying that I write neither in French nor in Creole. I write in Maryse Condé.

I realize now that I have never really clarified this point.

Let us never forget that Francophone literature from the Caribbean emerged after a long silence, after a long stretch of time during which the native islander was considered a disastrous parasite. He was deprived of his deepest inner self, forced to express himself in a foreign tongue and look at his own reality with borrowed eyes. Travellers and missionaries were the only ones who carried any weight. Their discourse was considered gospel truth on which was built a luxuriant island paradise disfigured precisely by the presence of its native islanders.

The song of Negritude initiated the process of exploration, then reappropriation, of the Caribbean universe and mankind. Nevertheless, Negritude remained mostly insensitive to the linguistic dispossession. In his *Notebook of a Return to My Native Land*, Césaire toyed with Latin and Greek words and thanks to them coined new rhythms and sounds.

Originally published as 'Liaison dangereuse' in Michel Le Bris and Jean Rouaud (eds), *Pour une littérature monde* (Paris: Gallimard, 2007), pp. 205–16.

If we think about it, the peoples of the Caribbean have never stopped losing their language. The descent into hell, deep in the holds of the slave ships, coincided with the elimination of the African languages. Since the Bambara rubbed shoulders with the Nago and the Wolof with the Kongo, the result was inevitably a painful silence. At the end of the nineteenth century, enrolment in the schools of the French Republic sanctioned the marginalization of Creole that had become the language of communication. The child who spoke Creole at school was humiliated, forced to wear a dunce's cap and made to stand in the yard. The Antillean, however, loves his Creole. It's his alter ego. It embodies his history. Forged in the universe of the plantation, it accompanied him during revolts and the attempts to regain his freedom. In this respect, we can but admire the power of the slave's spirit which countered the negative assertions churned out against him. He transformed this prison universe, created for producing barrels of sugar and richly rewarding the white masters, into a laboratory out of which came a religion, a music and a language that would serve to convey a rich oral literature still alive. From there to endowing the Creole language with a singular expressiveness is but a short step. Its status is heightened even more so by its exclusion from every cultural institution. Those who write in Creole, therefore, are immediately taken to heart by a society which believes them to be closer to their island and thus praises them to the skies.

In order to illustrate this formidable bias, I shall give two examples. The white Creole, Saint-John Perse, was forgiven his mestiza nurse who smelt of the castor bean, his pale and beautiful mother under her heavy straw hat and his domestics with faces the colour of papaya and boredom, in short, his disdainful and scornful vision of

Guadeloupe *because* he was able to recall in Creole the 'kako bean'. Conversely, some wanted to go so far as to exclude Césaire, the founding father of our writing, from the domain of Martinican literature because he had ignored the sounds and rhythm of the Creole language.

I have described in *Tales from the Heart* how I grew up in a family who idolized French. My father worshipped it like you worship a woman. My mother, whose mother could neither read nor write, even less speak French, considered it the magic key that opened every door to social success. Every evening, instead of telling us the traditional tales of Zamba and Rabbit, she would recite to us verses by Victor Hugo, a poet for whom I still have a particular aversion. During their stays in Paris, my parents were particularly mortified when the *garçons de café* went into raptures over the way they spoke French. 'We're as much French as they are,' my father would sigh, sadly forgetting one important detail—his very blackness.

It's true that in those days black was not yet a cheap colour, according to Nicolás Guillén.[1] We were a long way from today's overcrowded schools cluttered with second-generation pupils of Arab, African and Caribbean descent. When I was in Paris with my parents, I was the only little Antillean at the nursery school on the rue Eblé in the seventh arrondissement and enjoyed a status of exception, of a prodigal child that would make every Negropolitan green with envy, a status reinforced further by my perfect elocution. 'She speaks so well!' the mistress used to say, smothering me with kisses.

---

1 See Nicolás Guillén, 'West Indies Ltd (1934)' in *Las grandes elegías y otros poemas* (Caracas, Venezuela: Biblioteca Ayacucho, 1984), pp. 3–11.

As you can guess, my position became extremely uncomfortable very early on. Not only did I speak French but I wrote it to perfection. In Guadeloupe, I was always top of my class. My compositions were read out by admiring teachers which guaranteed me an annoying reputation with the other children whose homework was striped in red ink—*Creolism, Creolism, Creolism*. Nevertheless, I constantly stole Creole from reliable servants who would not report my mischief to my parents. But the servants' language was as rudimentary as their lives. I needed a teacher. Where could I find one when I was cut off from everywhere that Creole flourished? In short, despite all my efforts, my linguistic exploits in Creole never improved right up to when I left Guadeloupe at the end of my teens. Fortunately, at the student hostel on the rue Lhomond, in the heart of Paris, I lived with a group of girls like myself, mostly Martinican, for whom French also served as a mother tongue. I shared a room with a gifted student of Spanish. Her god was Guillén whom we sometimes passed by in the Latin Quarter with his mop of silver hair. She could recite entire poems of his:

> *Las canas-largas-tiemblan*
> *De miedo ante la mocha.*
> *Quema el sol y el aire pesa. Gritos de mayorales*
> *Restellan secos y duros como foetes.*[2]

Playing records by Isaac Albéniz, she never missed an opportunity to explain her preference for the language of Cervantes, superior in every way to that of Molière. I listened to her without saying a word for I was incapable of arguing the contrary. My attachment to French was

2 Ibid., p. 5.

coupled with a curious feeling of bitterness towards it. Like a child adopted by a wealthy family who knows full well that her biological mother is vegetating in poverty and exclusion. At the same time, I was drawing attention to myself by writing in student rags and being admired for my articles. I hadn't yet dared to think of becoming a writer. However, I did see myself as a journalist. I remember two articles I wrote which caused quite a stir in our little circle. One was an enthusiastic review of *Compère Général Soleil* (1955) by Haitian novelist Jacques Stephen Alexis;[3] the other a virulent criticism of *Black Skin, White Masks* by Fanon whom I accused of not understanding our Antillean society. It's true, I'm not inventing anything.

In fact, my years of linguistic peace and happiness coincide with my years in Africa. Gone was the conflict between French and Creole. In Guinea, I followed my first husband, the director of the National Theatre, far into the back country to look for talented actors and texts. The latter were written in the national languages of which I did not know a word. In order to compensate for my ignorance, I conscientiously learnt Malinké. To speed things up, I would listen to the great griot Kouyate Sory Kandian and I didn't miss a single concert by the Instrumental Ensemble. Alas, these years came to an end and I had to return to Guadeloupe where, wiser for my experience, I joined forces with the Guadeloupean independence movement. The problems of Guinea and Ghana, where I had previously lived, were certainly different from those of Guadeloupe. As a first-hand witness, however, I had seen

3 Available in English as: *General Sun, My Brother* (Carrol F. Coates trans.) (Charlottesville: University of Virginia Press, 1999).

the revolutionary flame waver, then be snuffed out by a dictator in both countries. I could help our independence movement avoid certain pitfalls and mistakes. At that time, the independence of Guadeloupe was very much on the agenda. *Lendependans!* It was in our dreams, little knowing that our dreams would never come true and that our decerebrated, disoriented island would be tied to a Europe that even the French did not want.

I hadn't anticipated, however, that the political debates and discussions would be held in Creole. My comrades in ideology spoke Creole ostentatiously and passionately, anxious to display by this symbolic choice their refusal of French domination. They even brought their children to the meetings, for it is never too early to spread the good word. They made it a point of honour to talk to them in Creole. I couldn't believe my ears. If I had dared speak to my parents in Creole I wonder what would have happened. But such an eventuality was unthinkable.

I never managed to laugh it all off. Wasn't this linguistic state of tension childish? Isn't a language a vehicle for other values besides the ones it conveys? Isn't it a simple medium? François Duvalier, who had no qualms about using Creole or putting on the habit of Baron Samedi, was the bloodiest dictator in the history of Haiti. Conversely, Louis Delgrès, before becoming a martyr by blowing himself up on the Danglemont plantation, wrote his famous 'Proclamation' (1802) in French, and what French!

> *A l'univers entier*
> *Le dernier cri de l'innocence et du désespoir*
> 'C'est dans les plus beaux jours d'un siècle à jamais célèbre par le triomphe des Lumières et de la philosophie qu'une classe d'infortunés qu'on

veut anéantir se voit obligée de lever la tête vers
la postérité . . .'

To the entire universe
The last cry of innocence and despair

'On one of the finest days of a century forever
famous for the triumph of the Enlightenment and
philosophy when a group of ill-fated wretches
they are bent on destroying are forced to raise
their heads to posterity . . .'[4]

I was right to polish my arguments for I was about to
publish *Heremakhonon*, my first novel, in 1976. I told myself
that the title in Malinké and the numerous references to
African orality ought to prove that I was open to every linguistic treasure. But I needn't have bothered. Those who
showed an interest in the book were too busy to bother
about my language, denigrating it for other reasons, not
the least of which was my challenging the sacrosanct
African revolution. I was not discouraged and wrote two
other books on Africa, a subject dear to me. I had learnt,
experienced and also suffered so much there. One of these
books afforded me a certain notoriety. Free from financial
worries for a time, I convinced my second husband to
come and live with me in Guadeloupe.

The island I came back to looked nothing like the
place I remembered. The perfect picture of modernity:
roads, four-lane highways, interchanges and somewhat
radiant housing projects. Although I made a pilgrimage to
Pointe-à-Pitre, to the house where I was born and grew up,
I chose to live in the country, in Montebello. From my

4 See Laurent Dubois, *A Colony of Citizens: Revolution and Slave Emancipation in the French Caribbean, 1787–1804* (Chapel Hill: The University
of North Carolina Press, 2004), pp. 391–2 (translation modified).

veranda, to the right, I had a view of the volcano, at times puffing angrily on its pipe; to the left, I could see the sea through a gap in the trees. Intellectually, matters soon began to take a less satisfying turn. Shortly after my arrival I was invited to a radio station of the independence movement for an important announcement. Rather than speak in bad Creole I chose to speak in French. I announced that I had managed to invite the African American novelist Paule Marshall and that such a visit was of the stuff required to reinforce this cultural unity of the Black World in which we so strongly believed. I spoke with passion. At the end of the programme, the station was flooded with questions from outraged listeners: Where did this Maryse Condé come from, who couldn't say a word in Creole?

It appeared that no one had paid any attention to the subject of my talk. Only the form. I realized that the war between Creole and French was not over. No, whatever I did, I would never be Sonny Rupaire with the prestigious aura of a draft dodger—he refused to fight against the Algerians and wrote in Creole. The poems from his *Cette igname brisée qu'est ma terre natale* (1971, This Broken Yam that is My Homeland) was on everyone's lips.[5]

Shortly afterwards, in 1989, the Créolité writers published their *Eloge de la Créolité*.[6] Invested with the authority

5 Sonny Rupaire, *Cette igname brisée qu'est ma terre natale* (Paris: Parabole, 1971).

6 Available in English as: Jean Bernabé, Patrick Chamoiseau, Raphaël Confiant, *Eloge de la Créolité. In Praise of Creoleness*, bilingual edn (Mohamed B. Taleb Khyar trans.) (Paris: Gallimard, 1993). Also available in *Callaloo* 13(4) (Autumn 1990): 886–909. All subsequent citations are from this latter source.

conferred by success, they narrowed the boundaries of Antillean literature.

Paradoxically, it was this pamphlet that for the first time made me ponder my relationship with the French language. I had not chosen this language. It had been given to me. Not by colonization. It would be absurd to think so. Colonization's role is to reduce the colonized to silence. It never gives anything to the peoples it has subjugated. Under pressure, it builds a few schools with the intention of training the subalterns it needs. The French language had been stolen by my loving parents and given to me so that I would be armed for life. I could no more question it than the colour of my eyes or the nature of my hair which they too had handed down to me. At all cost I had to rid myself of the guilty conscience I had every time I used French. I was only very recently able to exorcize these feelings completely when I wrote *Victoire, My Mother's Mother*. In this book I have endeavoured to explain the complex relationship between my mother and grandmother, all that had gone before which influenced my comportment. Nevertheless, I was never as happy as when I made peace with the French language because I was free to take stock of the treasure I unwittingly possessed. How I would have liked to be a poet or a cabaret singer to bend the rebellious tongue to my will! Raymond Queneau? Raymond Devos? Or griot, in order to combine words with music and rhythm? Jean-Jacques Rousseau was right: the written word is lifeless. We have to restore its lost warmth and to do so I experimented with a thousand stratagems.

It was then that I was invited to teach at the University of California at Berkeley. I'll take this opportunity to elucidate my reasons for leaving for the USA and settling there, for which I have often been criticized.

I was at a dead end. I could see full well that my books did not correspond to people's expectations and had little chance of attracting media attention, without which there is no chance of literary success. In fact, the rare critics who had shown interest in my last book lectured me on why I didn't imitate the Créolité writers. At a practical level, I had not found a job in Guadeloupe and my royalties were dwindling dangerously. And then to live in the USA does not mean making a pact with capitalism. The USA is full of people who contest Washington's politics and try to oppose it.

At Berkeley, there wasn't yet a Francophone programme but a programme of 'emerging literatures' where they studied, pell-mell, Jacques Roumain, Mariama Bâ and Sony Labou Tansi. Despite its risky title, the programme demonstrated the vitality of literatures in French. Voices were rising from just about everywhere, from Benin, Congo and Haiti. I realized just how much the end of the twentieth century belonged to us, the descendants of those they thought they had sentenced to silence. We could compare the French language to a fornicator never tired of sowing his wild oats with partners of many different origins.

I also realized the hidden power of a language. My French erected a virtual barrier between the Americans and me, even between the African Americans whom I first called 'brothers and sisters'. They did not consider me one of theirs. Blinded by their own experiences they made no attempt to understand mine which were not quite the same. They levelled my identity, treating me like a Frenchwoman. Africa had already whispered to me this intuition. Race is a signifier that doesn't signify very much unless it rests on strong foundations such as religion, a specific history or language. Before I came to live in the USA, I recall having written for some journal or other an article that poked fun at language, minimizing its importance. I put it down to the whims of fate. My ancestors had been captured by one slave trader rather than another and sold into the possession of the king of France. How mistaken I was! Language is a binding, mysterious and powerful tie which is colour-blind. *Lyannaj*, they say in Guadeloupe.

As I said, I write in Maryse Condé because, like a miser who has no intention of sharing his treasure, I do not want to share the French language with anyone. It has been forged for me alone. For my personal delectation. What does it matter if others have used it before me and others will use it after me! I don't care what use others make of it, strangers for all I care, whether they are called Marcel Proust or Léopold Sédar Senghor!

So perhaps I am not a real Francophone writer.

Searching for Our Truths

> Not a piece of this world that does not bear my
> fingerprint
> And my calcaneus on the backs of skyscrapers and
> my filth in the glitter of gems.
>
> Aimé Césaire, *Notebook of a Return to My Native Land*

I have no inclination whatsoever to talk about myself.

After ten novels and almost twenty years of writing, I picture myself as déjà vu or saying the same old things, whatever you like. I prefer to talk about what I deem necessary at the end of our twentieth and the beginning of our twenty-first century. I'd like to talk about a redefinition of 'Caribbean literature'. Fifty years ago, we recall Césaire arrogantly stating in his *Notebook* that he belonged to none of the nationalities provided for by the chancelleries. I am wondering whether this is not the case for most of us today and if the old notions of race, nationality and territory to which we cling are not becoming obsolete.

A hundred years ago, it was fairly simple to define a Guadeloupean, a Martinican or a Haitian. First of all, they were born in their island. This might seem a statement of

Originally published as 'Chercher nos vérités' in Madeleine Cottenet-Hage and Maryse Condé (eds), *Penser la Créolité* (Paris: Karthala, 1995), pp. 305–10.

the obvious. It is important, however, since, according to demographers, 85 per cent of us never left our native land. At birth, the midwife buried the placenta under a tree in the garden and it consequently became one's double. On death, they were buried under the casuarinas in the village graveyard in a grave lined by conches, whitewashed with quicklime. Most of them spoke only Creole, the pidgin born in the plantation system that became their mother tongue. They hardly spoke French since schooling averaged five or six years. Their literature was mostly oral and in Creole.

Today, everything is much more complex. First of all, Guadeloupe and Martinique have become host islands for immigrants. Thousands of Haitians and Dominicans from Dominica and the Dominican Republic have settled there, each bringing a little of their culture. Secondly, demographers tell us that only 30 per cent of Caribbean people have never left their island. For the others, life is a succession of comings and goings between their own islands and France as well as any of the other European countries where work is available. When they return to the island, there is a marked change in their comportment which is imparted subtly to the rest of society. Finally, over half a million Guadeloupeans and Martinicans reside permanently in France. Their children, named Second Generation by the immigration experts, no longer resemble them, speaking like their little French classmates with little knowledge, thank goodness, of that Antillean accent that swallowed the *r*s mentioned by Fanon. They seldom read but spend hours watching Japanese and American cartoons on television. Their only contact with the actual Caribbean is incidental, when they spend their summer holidays, sometimes accompanied by their parents, with their grandmothers or aunts who have stayed on the island. Or when they are grown up and take Caribbean literature classes with a specialist. My classes at Nanterre University and Paris IV attracted a great many of these nostalgic students. This schema of transplantation and uprooting I have just described applies to every island of the Caribbean whether they are English-speaking, Spanish-speaking or Dutch-speaking. London, Liverpool, Amsterdam, New York and Miami each have their neighbourhoods where Caribbean people are practically the only community. This schema is somewhat more complicated as regards the Haitians. A million Haitians live in North America (Canada and the USA). An equal number have migrated to Europe. This results in some surprising linguistic combinations: the young Haitians in New York or Toronto have managed to keep their Creole but have lost their French and speak in English. Danticat, for example, transplanted to Brooklyn at the age of eight, wrote her first novel in English. I have seen young Haitians in Cologne and Amsterdam speaking neither French nor Creole but only German or Dutch.

Generally speaking, these immigrant communities are looked down upon by the Caribbean people who have remained at home. People poke fun at their accent as well as their inability to speak perfect Creole. Their culture, kept alive through numerous associations, is rejected and marginalized because it does not correspond to the standard definition of authentic. They are given derisory nicknames. The Guadeloupeans and Martinicans living in France are called Negropolitans or Negzagonals. The only area where immigrant culture has managed to impose itself is music, for everyone conveniently forgets that the somewhat over-celebrated *zouk* music first found its roots in the suburbs of Paris.

At the same time, it is not only Caribbean identity which is changing dimensions but also European identity. A few months ago, a television documentary entitled *Poor Whites*, shot in Guadeloupe by E. René-Corail, made the headlines. Apart from its imperfections, it had the extraordinary merit of portraying the increasing number of Europeans who come to while away their life under the Caribbean sun. It would be easy to rule them off as dropouts. Although drugs largely continue to offer easy access to paradise for many of them, this new species of Europeans testifies to the collapse of the old social pyramid. The whites—as defined in the film's ironic title—are no longer represented by the arrogant planter, the owner of slaves and of great houses on top of the hill. He is no longer even the civil servant counting on his 40 per cent cost-of-living increase to buy an apartment for his retirement in his hometown back in France. He can be a former city dweller tired of the constraints of industrialized society. He can be unemployed. He can even be homeless. And the anger of the white Creoles and the metropolitan French civil servants, deeply wounded in their pride as a class and a race, joins hands with the terror of the coloured Antilleans who want the colonial conventions to stay as they are, who want to continue to hate the white man and make him responsible for all the evils of their society and who will not admit that slavery is over.

Caribbean literature at the end of the twentieth century has not taken into account this upheaval, these transformations and redefinitions of *identity*. Admittedly, the only voices we hear are those of writers living in the islands. We take delight in noting that all of them have been Negropolitans or Negzagonals for some period in their life. Nevertheless, they conveniently forget that and defend a definition of the Antillean Creole worthy of the times when Lady Nugent visited Jamaica (around 1839). Paradoxically, in order to convince themselves of the 'authenticity' they portray of their native island in their writings, they boast of their success in French literary circles which are always on the lookout for new exoticisms. 'The interactional or transactional aggregate' which everyone admits is at the basis of the Antillean cultural phenomenon is not petrified like lava on the side of a volcano. It is a constant magma. On a linguistic level, the Antilleans can no longer remain prisoners of the binary opposition: Creole versus French, which is but a legacy of the colonial obsession between victor and victim. Erroneously revolutionary, this linguistic dichotomy is in fact backward-looking and denies the fundamental discoveries of order and societal power implied in every language. We are surprised that Confiant criticizes Césaire for not having written in Creole. Doesn't he know that a writer endeavours to find his language well beyond mother or foreign tongue? Césaire has forged his own speech; that's all that matters. As Wilson Harris says for the writer: 'Language itself is the ground of an interior and active expedition through and beyond what is already known.'[1]

Where lies the Caribbean today? A place with no defined limits, porous to every distant rumour, traversed by every kind of influence, even contradictory. Rap rubs shoulders with the *gwoka*. Vaudeville theatre with traditional wake ceremonies. The oral poetry in Creole by Max Rippon with the poetry of Aimé Césaire and Derek

1 Wilson Harris, *Fossil and Psyche* (Austin: University of Texas at Austin, Occasional Publications, African and Afro-American Studies Research Center, 1974), p. 9.

Walcott. Cultural elements from every direction collide, bleed into each other and give birth to new forms. We must place greater value on the new forms of cultural hybridity which challenge the traditional ones already stratified by usage. Hybridity has always terrorized established societies who want to protect their women from the sperm of foreign males and, consequently, from any change.

Change terrifies. Through his literature, the Antillean exorcizes his fear of the future and convinces himself of the continuity of the present.

Caribbean literature, however, has always wanted to be the expression of a community. Writing was meant to be a collective act. Even when he says 'I', the Caribbean writer is supposed to think 'we'. Bernabé, Chamoiseau and Confiant decree rules for men of letters. Our writing, they command, 'must look for our truths. One of its *missions* is to present insignificant heroes, anonymous heroes, those who are forgotten by the colonial chronicle, those who resisted indirectly and patiently and who have nothing in common with the Western or French heroes' (my emphasis).[2]

We could spend a long time analysing this text to demonstrate that it is a faithful translation of the colonial obsession we have already denounced. Let us retain merely the first sentence: 'It must look for our *truths*' (my emphasis).

What are these truths at the end of the twentieth century? And what have we become?

Already, part of Haitian literature is written in English; another in French but in Quebec. Part of English-speaking Caribbean literature is taking root in London and its

2 Bernabé, Chamoiseau and Confiant, 'In Praise of Creoleness', pp. 897–8.

suburbs. Axel Roehmer, a writer from Surinam, lives in The Hague and publishes in Amsterdam. The Caribbean writer is no longer a native of his island and therefore no longer Creole as it was understood in the eighteenth century meaning . . . or in *In Praise of Creoleness*. Aren't there not multiple versions of Caribbeanness? And new meanings of Créolité?

Or perhaps we should quite simply meditate on the words of Harris in *The Four Banks of the River of Space* (1990): 'When one dreams, one dreams alone. When one writes a book, one is alone.'[3]

3 Wilson Harris, *The Four Banks of the River of Space* (London: Faber and Faber, 1990), p. 4.

The Voyager In, the Voyager Out

I never knew my grandmother, Sylvère, *bonne-maman*, who died long before I was born. I know very little about her. I do know, however, every detail of a journey she made to Morne Vert in Martinique when she was about sixteen to the christening of her aunt's baby (the aunt, her mother's sister, had married a Martinican, something very rare at the time). It is proof that this short, modest trip had provided material for a mythical journey that was more essential and more traumatic than the largely eclipsed Middle Passage and more likely to make an impression on my family's collective imagination. This sort of founding myth unfolded in three parts. First, the crossing of a channel, then a stretch of ocean that was described as 'mountainous' and wild during which my future grandmother threw up her soul and her stomach over the ship's rail in the midst of an enormous cacophony. At her feet were piles of crates of black, squealing piglets, cackling chicken and bleating goats. Then there was the arrival at Fort-de-France, at dusk. Sylvère, who in all her life had never left La Treille, a rural district on the very rural island of Marie-Galante, had to make do with the *lakou* yard in Terres-Sainville where her aunt's

Originally published, with the same title, in Marie Abraham and Daniel Maragnès (eds), *Guadeloupe: Temps Incertains* (Paris: Autrement, 2001), pp. 250–9.

in-laws lived. At that time, Terres-Sainville was a gigantic shanty town, sprawling down its hill like a Brazilian *favela* into which were crammed jumbles of families and their brood. Children were crying, mothers were scolding them. Under the calabash trees, men were playing the *gwoka* drums which in Martinique they called *bel-air*. Sylvère was not used to such promiscuity and noise. Over dinner, round a dish of root vegetables, the Martinicans poked fun at her Guadeloupean accent and she went to bed in tears.

The third and final chapter of her journey took place the following day. After a cup of chocolate hastily downed in the early hours of the morning, she ran to catch the charabanc in the pouring rain, the likes of which she had never seen. When she arrived, she discovered that the buckets of water that were soaking Fort-de-France had not spared Morne Vert. They had washed down the gullies and dragged along torrents of mud that now buried half the neighbourhood. Two deaths were being mourned. Miraculously, her aunt's cabin was intact and her home spared. But the christening was stained with the colour of mourning. In other words, in forty-eight hours, Sylvère had come up against alterity, death and fatality. Back home, she swore she would never travel again. A few years later, solely in the interest of schooling her only daughter, my mother, she resigned herself to leave Marie-Galante and go and live in La Pointe.

Customs change with the times! My life, on the contrary, has been placed under the sign of travel.

I shall call attention, however, to only one instance, a journey I never chose to make and that I made long before I was born. Its memory still haunts me despite the centuries that separate us. I spent several days in a dark, airless fort.

Then they threw me into the hold of a ship that pitched and rolled towards an unknown destination. In the dark I lay, soaking in my urine and excrement. Once a week, sailors kicked and shoved me onto the deck to dance for exercise. The glare of the ocean that stretched as far as the eye could see hurt my eyes. The journey seemed unending. Finally, one morning, we reached a radiant and colourful land which at first sight consoled me for all the suffering and humiliation I had endured.

Undoubtedly, I had only dreamt this journey. Even so, it is the reason behind most of my journeys—no longer imaginary but real. It weighs with all its might on my unconscious and affects my imagination and creativity. For years this journey was the cause of my obsession with BEFORE, what went on BEFORE *Jesus Christ the King* set off from the shores of Africa and sailed to the New World with its sad cargo of men and women? What people were mine? How were they governed? What were their customs? What did they teach the children at a time when foreign values had not stifled most of their traditions like epiphytes on the trees in the dense forest? These questions, which explain my return to my roots in Mother Africa, as the saying goes, are the subject of my first two books: *Heremakhonon* and *A Season in Rihata* ([1981] 1988).[1] They were written on my experience in Guinea. Emerging from the family cocoon, I was not prepared for so much poverty, distress and destitution that endured in the midst of the revolutionary jargon. Above all, I had no idea of the dire consequences for a people constantly struggling to survive.

1 Maryse Condé, *A Season in Rihata* (Richard Philcox trans.) (Portsmouth, NH: Heinemann Educational Books, Caribbean Writers Series, 1988).

The material prevailed over all other considerations. No ideology, no virtue and no ideal could resist the desire to obtain a few banknotes. I therefore soon came to the conclusion: however much I travelled these countries I would never obtain the answers I was looking for. Drained by years of colonization and soon by dictatorship, and endeavouring with a thousand stratagems to worm their way into what they thought to be modernity, they could only accentuate my questioning.

I was about to bow out when quite by chance I came across Mali. I have often told the story of how this first journey as a tourist along the cities of the Niger Bend was a revelation to me. In season, when the waters were high, we boarded the boat at Gao, capital of the Askias, and slowly drifted upriver to Bamako. The banks of the river of an evening emerged out of a pinkish mist. I was disappointed by Timbuktu; it was nothing but a city of dust turned to dust, here and there bristling with the grey tumuli of bread ovens. In the Sankoré mosque district, the memory of its expert Arabic scholars and great marabouts had long vanished. Mopti, however, and especially Djenné, enthralled me. I was not only dazzled by the ochre splendour of its mosque, whose picture has been reproduced throughout the world, but I also discovered the elegant architecture of mud brick designed by the famous masons, the *bari*. I wandered along alleyways thronging with children, cripples and loaded mules. Suddenly, I thought I could guess what the past must have been like and also the reasons for its decline. So if Djenné had delighted me so much, why had I chosen in 1984 to write about Segu which is devoid of beauty? Precisely for that reason. In the twentieth century, this once powerful kingdom, cramped inside its mud walls, was a shadow of what it had once been. It was nothing more than a colonial *sous-préfecture*, bearing the scars of all those struggles from which we emerged defeated. Conquered. A group of *Talibés* in white boubous showed me the common graves where they had thrown the 'fetishists' pell-mell, executed by the Muslims in their jihad. And for good measure they then showed me the square where they used to behead the agitators in the pay of El Hadj Umar Tall.

Considered a celebration of Africa, *Segu* is above all a farewell, the renouncement of my quest for what went on BEFORE. Henceforth, I would deliberately erase the images that haunted me—of tall flames swallowing up straw huts, villages razed to the ground and chained captives marching into the open jaws of the slave ships anchored in the suffocating heat of a bay—in order to confront the present. I have never denied Africa's role as a common underlying substratum behind the cultural unity of the Caribbean. On an ideological level, however, I turned my back on the ideals of Pan-Africanism but without ever denying my admiration for Césaire. I distanced myself from Negritude. For me, now, the plantation system served as a matrix. The plantation, a trading sector, a place of material profit destined to produce barrels of sugar, served as a cultural laboratory, in spite of itself. Different ethnic groups, languages, religions and modes of thought rubbed shoulders and intermingled, producing a Caribbean syncretism.

As Chamoiseau and Confiant say quite rightly:

This tool for conquering and ground clearing, this machine for exploiting and enriching (that had never meant to lay down roots) developed a facet that none of its protagonists had either foreseen or desired: a culture, i.e. a universal response to

the situation, a vision of the world, a philosophy
of life, customs, together with a language common to us all: Creole.[2]

In order to better understand the manifestations of
this culture that I unknowingly carried in me, I was not
merely content to return to Guadeloupe. I journeyed many
times through the Caribbean, travelling patiently from
island to island. The beauty of the landscapes undeniably
enriched my writing. Jamaica, for example, figures largely
in *Tree of Life* published in 1988 [1987].[3] Far more than
Negril or Montego Bay, I can remember Cockpit Country,
that wild and rugged land of the Maroons. It is as if the
very soul of these rebels had imbued the mountains and
gullies of their former home. In the village of Nannytown,
a grave next to the church claimed to contain the remains
of the fighting rebel, now a national heroine. History
combines with legend. Guides had visitors admire the nar-
row gorge from where the British soldiers had been
ambushed with flaming branches. I roamed the Great
Houses, haunted, they say, as soon as night falls by the
ghosts of their dead masters, their hands still dripping with
the blood of their slaves. Santo Domingo was dominated
by the memory of Diégo Colón and the conquistadors.
Melancholic vessels, their hulls rusty from inaction, lay
dormant at the mouth of a river. In Dominica, gaunt, pale
children of the last of the Amerindians begged for money
from passers-by. Apart from these marvels, however, the

2 See Patrick Chamoiseau and Raphaël Confiant, *Lettres creoles.
Tracées antillaises et continentales de la literature. 1635–1975* (Paris:
Hatier, 1991).

3 Maryse Condé, *Tree of Life: A Novel of the Caribbean* (Victoria Reiter
trans.) (New York: Ballantine Books, 1988).

Caribbean seemed to me characterized above all by its diversity. How can we compare Haiti, crowded with eponymous heroes, glorying in the first successful slave revolution and midwife of myths, with Guadeloupe that has known only abortive struggles? How can we compare Cuba, a splinter driven into the heart of the USA, with Puerto Rico, regularly promised to be raised to the blessed rank of fifty-first state? Or Jamaica with its Maroons and Rastas with Barbados that boasts of its nickname Little England? Besides the hurricanes that wreak havoc on every island with equal ferocity, the coconut trees, the royal palms dear to Saint-John Perse and here and there the echo of drums, everything seemed different at first sight. Gradually, however, I was instilled with the secret unity forged by a common history and ethnicity. Jamaica, Cuba, Puerto Rico and the entire Caribbean have gone through four identical centuries of change and turbulence and lived through the experience of slavery, trauma and chaos. This mismatched mosaic, now at last a people, was sung by Guillén as early as 1934:

> Here are whites, blacks, Chinese and Mulattoes,
> A series of cheap colours, are they not,
> Where after so many deals and contracts
> The colours have run and not one is dyed fast.[4]

Almost fifty years later, Antonio Benítez-Rojo tried to systematically elucidate this unity in *The Repeating Island* (1992).[5] As for me, searching for a kind of easily identifiable

---

4 Guillén, 'West Indies Ltd' in *Las grandes elegías y otros poemas*, p. 3.

5 See Antonio Benítez-Rojo, *The Repeating Island: The Caribbean and the Postmodern Perspective* (James E. Maraniss trans.) (Durham, NC: Duke University Press, 1992).

uniformity, it slipped away and hid under the official history, the political status to which I attached too much
importance and the complacent discourse of the societies
about themselves and the image they wanted to convey.
The concept of culture is a legacy of eighteenth-century
philosophy and Enlightenment anthropology, and has been
subjected to a number of meaningful variations. Today,
ethnologists, especially French ethnologists, have popular-
ized a notion of culture that can be compared to a chef's
recipe. In *The Video Diary*, shot during a recent trip to Mali
with African American actor Danny Glover,[6] Manthia
Diawara, the author of *In Search of Africa* (1998), deplores
the way Dogon culture has been ossified, reified, and the
voice of Ogotemmêli become the transcendent, unchang-
ing and univocal mouthpiece.[7] Fanon's warning of a culture's subterranean, perpetually moving, indeed elusive,
nature has never been able to topple Marcel Griaule's
authority. The attempt to define a culture boils down to
freezing it in one of its fleeting moments. A culture has to
be felt and lived—that's all that matters.

The declaration by Haitian poet Anthony Phelps at
'Moi, écrivain des Amériques' (1981, I, Writer of the Americas), a conference in Padua, in which he refuses to be a
writer with a prefix—African American, Negro-African—
radiated in those years like a flash of blasphemy.[8] Coming

6 *Diaspora Conversations: From Goree to Dogon. A Video Diary by Manthia
Diawara.* Produced, directed and written by Manthia Diawara. Distributed by Third World Newsreel, New York. 2000. 47 mins.

7 See Manthia Diawara, *In Search of Africa* (Cambridge, MA: Harvard
University Press, 1998).

8 See Anthony Phelps, 'Littérature Negro-Africaine d'Amerique:
mythe ou réalité', *Ethiopiques* [new series] 1(3–4) (1983): 15–24.

well before the famous declaration of identity in *In Praise of Creoleness*: 'Neither Europeans, nor Africans, nor Asians, we proclaim ourselves Creoles,'[9] this bold step began the decentring of Africa which was to take shape in later years. Soon, like many others, I questioned the very notion of diaspora, fearing that it contained the concept of a mystical attachment to the so-called land of origin and hence a spiritual or physical return which ran counter to enhancing the image of the new environment of the Caribbean.

A new interrogation, however, soon emerged to trouble the serenity of these half-certainties. Okay, Caribbean culture existed; it could be a source of pride by proving that the slave was not a brute. But where does the Caribbean begin and end? Must we restrict it to the islands of the archipelago? Should we acknowledge the 'Caribbean coast' of Colombia? Concede six degrees of Caribbeanness to Venezuela? And what about the South of the USA?

I have often told the story about the time in December 1989, when, after having taught a semester as visiting professor at the University of Virginia, I decided to drive down to Miami for my return to Guadeloupe. Shortly before nightfall I entered Charleston whose splendour friends had told me about. To my amazement the town was partially destroyed, its mansions and town houses collapsed or in repair, covered with blue tarps. It looked as though an enemy had ruthlessly attacked this architectural marvel without distinction. 'It's the hand of Hugo!' I was told in answer to my distress. Of course I knew Hugo. A few months earlier, the terrible hurricane had practically levelled Guadeloupe before continuing on its path to sow desolation elsewhere. It was then that I had the intuition

9 Bernabé, Chamoiseau, Confiant, 'In Praise of Creoleness', p. 886.

that we had to expand the notion of the Caribbean. As Édouard Glissant reminds us:

> The Plantation stretched its same principles of structure from the South of the United States and the Caribbean to the Caribbean shores of Latin America and Northeast Brazil. We must try to understand why, in regions linguistically so different and involved in such disparate political dynamics, the same organization governs economic production and establishes a way of life.[10]

I was well aware of the links between Barbados and the Carolinas at the time of slavery. I knew that the French planters fleeing the revolution in Santo Domingo had found refuge in Louisiana. This relatively unique example, however, of a culture determined by a common history and system of exploitation was conveyed to me by its geographical environment and natural phenomena. This revelation abounded in consequences. Now captivated, I returned to Charleston several times. I also travelled to Savannah and the Sea Islands, a string of isles off the shore of Georgia where the black people still speak in Gullah, a language inherited from their African ancestors. American modernity to a large extent has deprived them of their mystery. Access is by an endless tarmac bridge. Yet between the beaches and the gated communities for millionaires, the half-abandoned hovels and graveyards still remain. All these geographical

10 Édouard Glissant, 'Identité racine, identité relation' in *Identité, culture, développement* (Paris: Editions caribéennes, 1992), pp. 199–204. Proceedings of an international colloquium organized in Pointe-à-Pitre by the Committee for Culture, Education and Environment in Guadeloupe, Guyana, Martinique and Réunion (11–13 December 1989).

journeys obviously translated into literature. The town of Charleston provides the backdrop for my novel *The Last of the African Kings* ([1992] 1997).[11] This place, undeniably marked by its past, its slave market, its harbour where slave ships used to anchor and its mansions with their pediments and columns, was perfectly suited to the exploration of the relationship between the diasporas as well as the ties it kept with Africa.

Transnationalism and globalization soon complicated this schema which was already by no means simple. Everyone knows that the end of the twentieth century has been marked by the phenomenon of migration. Caribbean migration is certainly nothing new. Jamaican historian Winston James has demonstrated in his book *Holding Aloft the Banner of Ethiopia* (1998) how, without Marcus Garvey, George Padmore and Sylvester Wiliams, the ideals of Pan-Africanism and the Back to Africa movement, which at a time shook America, would never have been born.[12] But today the phenomenon of migration is on the increase. Demographers tell us that there are more Caribbean people than African Americans in the state of New York. Every major city in Canada houses large communities of people from the Caribbean. There is a joke that every Jamaican writer lives in . . . Toronto. Canada sets an example by granting citizenship to Emile Ollivier from Haiti, Neil Bissoondath from Trinidad and Michael Ondaatje from Sri Lanka. It doesn't think it cultural imperialism or abusive assimilation; rather, it is a recognition of the fact that these

11 Maryse Condé, *The Last of the African Kings* (Richard Philcox trans.) (Lincoln: University of Nebraska Press, 1997).

12 See Winston James, *Holding Aloft the Banner of Ethiopia*: *Caribbean Radicalism in America, 1900–1932* (London: Verso, 1998).

writers from elsewhere not only contribute to the national genius but also subtly modify and influence it. The classic question which tacitly positions them in a relationship of dependence vis-à-vis the canon consists in asking Caribbean writers what works have influenced them. It would be interesting to turn the question round and ask a writer from Montreal, Quebec, Miami, Baltimore or Paris what changes the contact with these 'foreigners' has had on their imagination and creativity. At a conference organized by the University of Maryland in 1992, French writer Marie Redonet complained that, because of the popularity of the Martinican writers, her editor blamed her for being too conventional in her language and ordered her to instil new life and energy into it. More recently, at a conference for black writers in Brooklyn, African American poet Quincy Troupe expressed his keen interest in literature from Guadeloupe and Martinique. What does this interest imply? Surely an intertextuality yet to be seen. If writing is in fact a relation between texts, then Caribbean writers are invited to dialogue with Troupe and express themselves. So, what journeys, people will quip, what explorations remain to be carried out to get to the end of my search for identity once and for all?

Like my grandmother Sylvère, at the end of such a different journey, I have decided to stay home. My wandering and nomadism are over!

Because I live in New York, the hybrid city par excellence, a laboratory where a new human being is forged and matured. Although the USA turns a blind eye to biological hybridity, although their official doctrine states that a person with a drop of black blood is in fact black, this obsolete principle is culturally refuted at every instant. New York is the city of the Fugees, Danticat, Díaz and García, in other words, a generation of artists who are living proof that the Caribbean imagination invades, transgresses and remodels cultural canons as it pleases. It mocks the place of expression and the language in which it speaks. It integrates and transcends every influence. It dies in one shape only to be reborn in another.

In fact, why should I be concerned any longer with what went on BEFORE when TOMORROW will be so beautiful?

Beyond Languages and Colours

If I had been born on some island to the north-west of the Caribbean archipelago, say Cuba or the Dominican Republic, I would be speaking Spanish. If I had been born a few islands to the south, such as Trinidad, I would be speaking English. Even farther south, but more to the west, in Curacao, I would be speaking Dutch or Papiamento. As chance would have it, the hazards of razzias, abductions and rapes of the slave trade meant that my ancestors, dazed by despair and blinded by the glare of daylight, emerged from the slave ship into the mangrove of a small island, Guadeloupe, a possession of the Catholic king of France.

To put it plainly, if the story of my ancestors had unfolded without conflict or trauma, today I would be speaking Bambara, Hausa or Yoruba. With a little luck, I would have grown up in one of the courtyards of the Oba's palace. I would be called Ayodele which means 'joy has come home.' I would be wearing wrappers dyed blue with indigo. Instead of that, here I am in front of you. My name is Maryse Condé and I am speaking to you in French. In a certain respect, every word of this language I speak ought to be a reminder of the historical defeat and the loss of identity my ancestors suffered. But let us be true to our-

Originally published as 'Au-delà des langues et des couleurs' in *La Quinzaine Littéraire* 436 (May 1985): 36.

selves and admit that I now live without remorse or suffering in the land of the French language.

How did I arrive at this point? My story is not simple but, rest assured, I will sum it up in very short sections.

1 / THE TIME OF CAREFREE INDIFFERENCE

The societies that established themselves in the Caribbean after the arrival of Columbus are characterized by the plantation system. The plantation was a complex place. Initially a simple space where the land was conquered and cleared, it soon became a laboratory for the elaboration of religious systems, such as voodoo in Haiti and Santeria in Cuba, as well as culinary and medical traditions. And, above all, for a linguistic system. It is a scientific fact that a pidgin becomes a Creole when one of its linguistic groups adopts it as mother tongue. The pidgin used for communication between the African slaves of different origins and their European masters gave birth to Creole and more and more Africans forgot their ethnic language.

The common belief, however, is that we, the children of the Caribbean, grew up with the sounds of Creole. We are surrounded by stereotypes. Our placentas are said to be buried under the mapou trees. Our mothers or grandmothers in cane bundlers' dress, similar to Joseph Zobel's Mama Tine in his *Black Shack Alley* ([1950] 1980),[1] cradling us in their arms deep into the cane fields, are supposed to have taught us the tales of Bre'er Rabbit, Zamba, Ti-Jean, the three-legged horse of the Bête à Man Hibè or Little Sapotille, carried over in the language of the defunct plantation.

1 Joseph Zobel, *Black Shack Alley* (Keith Q. Warner trans.) (Washington, DC: Three Continents Press, 1980).

The reality is quite different. Urban families living a European way of life like mine had long turned their backs on Creole. Concerned with social ascension, they forbade their children to speak what they called a 'jargon of the ill-educated'. They had managed to appropriate the French language and were proud of it. There was an extraordinary power in possessing the language of the former master. The subaltern could thus grow closer to his former master and become his equal. In order to illustrate my childhood years, here are a few lines from the poem 'Hoquet' (1937) by Léon-Gontran Damas, one of the Negritude poets:

> Be quiet
> Didn't I tell you you had to speak French
> The French of France
> The French of the French
> French French.[2]

At the same time, the education we received at the *lycée* was modelled on that of France. Classes were taught in French. Creole was forbidden. We were as familiar with Corneille, Racine and Molière as we were with every detail of Napoleon's battles. We didn't know, of course, that he had re-established slavery in the French possessions and that in 1802, in a letter to his brother-in-law, General Victor-Emmanuel Leclerc, he wrote with contempt of François-Dominique Toussaint Louverture and Jean-Jacques Dessalines, the heroes of Haitian independence: 'Rid us of these gilded Africans and our desires will be fulfilled.'[3]

2 Léon-Gontran Damas, 'Hoquet' in *Pigments / Névralgies* (1937) (Paris: Présence Africaine, 1972), p. 38.

3 'Bonaparte to Leclerc' (1 July 1802) in Jean-Baptiste Vaillant (ed.), *Correspondance de Napoléon, Ier, publiée par ordre de l'empereur Napoléon III*, VOL. 7, p. 640.

In short, for many long years, right up to the end of our teens, the island did not hold an identity for us. It was merely a décor of palm trees, sea and beaches of white or grey sand. We had no idea it possessed a culture. We hadn't yet read Hegel. We doubted, however, that it possessed a history. As Glissant writes in his *Caribbean Discourse* (1989), our collective memory was perfectly erased.[4] All we dreamt of was crossing the Atlantic to discover what lay on the other side.

At that time I was already dreaming of becoming a writer. Needless to say, I chose without hesitation my masters among the great names of French literature, the only one I knew. My idol was François Mauriac.

2 / THE TIME OF A PAINFUL QUEST

In 'The Lived Experience of the Black Man', Chapter 5 of *Black Skin, White Masks*, Fanon reminds us of the Antillean's trauma when he is obliged to leave his island and confront the gaze of the white man: 'I was responsible not only for my body but also for my race and my ancestors. I cast an objective gaze over myself, discovered my blackness, my ethnic features; deafened by cannibalism, backwardness, fetishism, racial stigmas, slave traders, and above all, yes, above all, the grinning *Y a bon Banania*.'[5]

These very posters that Senghor dreamt of ripping off the walls of France.

We have all lived Fanon's experience to some degree or another. Hardly has he set foot in Europe than the myth

4 Édouard Glissant, *Caribbean Discourse: Selected Essays* (J. Michael Dash ed. and trans.) (Charlottesville: University of Virginia Press, 1989).

5 Fanon, *Black Skin, White Masks*, p. 92.

of France, the mother country, collapses for the Antillean. The sudden realization of alterity is painful. In my disappointment, I plunged into the poets of the Negritude movement. At the time of which I am speaking, at the beginning of the 1960s, although, as I have just said, I knew Baudelaire, Rimbaud and Mallarmé inside out, I had never heard the name of Césaire nor of the poets of the Caribbean. I delved, therefore, into their calls for back to Africa, the mother country, the matrix of all black peoples. I learnt of the existence of the great black universities in Djenné and Sankoré as well as African spirituality. I gorged myself on books on ethnology and history. As soon as I arrived in France, I began to ask myself unorthodox questions such as: Wasn't the famous sixteenth-century 'pyramid' dividing noble languages, attached to a long tradition of literature, and the others, the common languages, tendentious? Likewise, the separation between written and oral languages or written and oral literature? Wasn't written language and literature too often assimilated with civilization? It was the first time I realized that a language could stop being a means of communication and become an instrument of oppression. I pondered Barthes's words: 'To rob a man of his language in the very name of language: this is the first step in all legal murders.'[6]

In short, for the first time, I questioned the French language and my relationship to it. I wondered whether the language I had spoken until then was really mine and even began to ask myself if it was not responsible for secretly mutilating me.

6 Roland Barthes, 'Dominici, or The Triumph of Literature' in *Mythologies* (Annette Lavers trans.) (New York: Hill and Wang, 1972), pp. 43–6; here, p. 46.

You should not be surprised at these belated questions. The linguistic issue is a secondary problem in the stages of the colonial process. It emerged very late in anti-colonial thought. During the Pan-African Congress in Manchester in 1945, neither Kwame Nkrumah, the Ghanaian leader, nor Jomo Kenyatta mention it whereas they talk extensively of other types of oppression, be they economic, social or political. Yet in the other camp, as early as 1492, Antonio de Nebrija, Bishop of Avila, had said to Queen Isabella of Spain that language was the perfect instrument of empire.

In 1832, Duke of Rovigo, on the subject of Algeria, went even further when he said that he considered the propagation of education and of his language the most efficient instrument for dominating this country. And that the true working wonder would be to gradually replace Arabic by French.[7]

In 1960, heeding the advice of the Negritude poets, I decided to travel the Middle Passage in reverse and go back to Africa, the place where I would apparently become reconciled with myself.

In my early novels, *Heremakhonon*, *A Season in Rihata* and *Segu*, I have tried to explain what I felt to be an extremely rewarding but sometimes painful pilgrimage to my origins. I shall merely sum it up here. At the end of a twelve-year reflection, I realized that I had not understood to the full Fanon's *Wretched of the Earth*:

> The only common denominator between the
> blacks from Chicago and the Nigerians or

7 Anne-Jean-Marie-René Savary, *Mémoires du Duc de Rovigo pour servir à l'histoire de l'empereur Napoléon* (Paris: Bossange et Charles Béchet, 1829).

Tanganyikans was that they all defined themselves in relation to the whites. But once the initial
comparisons had been made and subjective
feelings had settled down, the black Americans
realized that the objective problems were funda-
mentally different [. . .] Negro or Negro-African
culture broke up because the men who set out to
embody it realized that every culture is FIRST
AND FOREMOST NATIONAL.[8]

He stated then what I had only just discovered—that
Culture prevails over Race.

On another level, at the level of my literary education,
those years in Africa were not lost. I realized in fact that I
had given too much priority to the written word. Orality
possessed unsuspected hidden treasures. Merging the spoken word with music, gesture and rhythm, the griots
revealed to me an art of communication I had never
known. In Paris, my revelation of Africa had been from
books. In the field, I saw it for myself. In my books I
endeavoured to capture this magic. I endeavoured to imitate the rhythm of the epic songs and the gentleness of the
lullabies. I inserted into my narratives fragments of traditional texts and proverbs. But they were never more than
somewhat clumsy translations and I felt like a copyist.

Then once again I was besieged with questions. Had
my island, a child of Africa, lost this art of the spoken word
which was now dazzling me in other places? Had I not
grown up deaf to its parlance? Was it really deprived of
culture and history as I believed? In other words, I needed
the encounter with Africa to shock me into questioning
my true identity.

8 Fanon, *The Wretched of the Earth*, pp. 153–4 (emphasis in the original).

3 / RETURN TO MY NATIVE LAND

Back home in Guadeloupe, after almost thirty years of absence, I discovered the cultural resistance of this little piece of land given over to the raging ocean and centuries of assimilation. Wiser for my experience of what I had heard in Africa, I opened my ears. The griots had long vanished. The storytellers at wake ceremonies had grown moribund. I made no effort to revive them. Yet I was struck by the complexity of daily speech, the term linguists call 'linguistic continuum'. In the French Antilles, every speaker travels along a linguistic line which goes from the most basilectal Creole to the least contaminated French. To parody Cuban poet Guillén, no sound is pure—all have been remodelled, reinterpreted and cannibalized. I wrote two novels illustrating this experience: *Tree of Life* and *Crossing the Mangrove* ([1989] 1995).[9] Yet what seems to me important is not merely that Creole words as well as metaphors inspired by the island's composite speech appear for the first time in my texts but that I tackled the very narrative structure. I endeavoured to imagine a structure that was not linear, that recreated the meanders and circumvolutions of Caribbean communication.

All round me, however, Guadeloupe and Martinique were ravaged by a genuine war. Neighbour was firing on neighbour. A hastily traced line of demarcation separated the advocates of a literature written in Creole or in a French largely deconstructed by Creole from those advocating a literature in French. Since Creole was considered the mother tongue, even for those who had never spoken it in their childhood (the individual is hateful, only the

9 Maryse Condé, *Crossing the Mangrove* (Richard Philcox trans.) (New York: Random House, 1995).

community counts), and since French, after four centuries
of appropriation, was supposed to remain the colonial language, the Creole speakers were declared children worthy
of the Caribbean and the French speakers traitors to the
collective identity. According to the terms of this somewhat unsubtle distinction, a number of would-be poets—
who otherwise would have been largely forgotten—found
themselves celebrities by virtue of the fact that they scrib-
bled in Creole. Césaire, in my opinion the founding mapou
tree of Antillean literature, was relegated to the camp of
traitors because he never lent his ear to the harmonies of
popular speech. His literature, like all Negritude literature,
was termed inauthentic. It was said to make no clear reading of beauty nor remedy the aesthetic confusion of the
Martinicans.

It was, I think, this criticism of Césaire which first
opened my eyes. First of all, I thought it puerile and revealing a profound ignorance of the colonial situation. What
intellectual, even in revolt, at the time of the Second World
War, would think of writing in the language of the subaltern? As we underlined previously, the linguistic dimension
of colonial oppression had hardly been explored. Césaire,
on the contrary, showed exceptional sensitivity to the linguistic problem by endeavouring to subvert the French language with neologisms, erudite words and, above all, by
breaking the straitjacket of grammar and syntax with the
use of automatic writing borrowed from the Surrealists.

The dichotomy, Creole versus French, mother tongue
versus colonial language, seemed to me inherited from the
colonial universe which likewise pitted master versus slave,
black versus white, free versus enslaved, nature versus
culture and civilized versus barbarian. I began to think
that we needed to invent a strategy for eradicating these

stereotyped conventions. Furthermore, with W. V. Humboldt, we had all believed that a language symbolized a certain vision of the world, and that to impose a language on someone amounts to aggressing him in his very intimacy. Without wanting to deny the power of linguistics, I wondered in the end whether Bakhtin was not right by insisting on the hybridity of languages. Bakhtin believes that depending on the speaker's ethnicity, social class and gender, language is a different signifier. It possesses what we call the power of double entendre. The French that I speak and write has little in common with the French from France. My ancestors stole it, like Prometheus stole fire, and passed it down to me. Can't I do what I like with it? Although it's a colonial language, haven't I colonized it in turn?

By this process of exclusion I realized that literary creation is born out of individual effort. Literature is plural. Every writer must seek out his path and voice alone based on his subjectivity and personal history. He must accept neither canon nor diktat imposed by the Other. He must refuse to confine himself to a school or follow the herd. To claim that an entire literary production is aligned on identical aesthetic criteria boils down to assassinating individual creativity. Furthermore, in a text, any linguistic or narrative inspiration that is repetitive becomes a system which is harmful to the sincerity of the act of creation. The writer must continue to surprise his reader and himself.

Césaire's Negritude, Senghor's Negritude

On 18 April 1971, the closing remarks were made at a conference on Negritude organized under the auspices of the Senegalese Progressive Union. Participants included Léopold Sédar Senghor himself, Léon-Gontran Damas, Mercer Cook, Maurice Piquion (representing Duvalier's Haiti) and other latecomers to Negritude, but no less motivated. One notable absence—Aimé Césaire.

This absence could have passed for accidental if Césaire, over the years, had not visibly lost interest in a concept that he had mainly instigated; now, the absence looked like the confirmation of a divorce. In fact, we should be talking about two Negritudes. Césaire's Negritude which seems to belong to the past and Senghor's Negritude which endeavours to shine far and wide and, thanks to the privileged political position of its great theoretician, strives for advancement to the rank of ideology for the Black World.

We shall not return to the distant origins of Negritude here and we shall not discuss either the Légitime Défense group or the Harlem Renaissance and *L'Étudiant noir*. These various movements have been studied in depth, notably by Lilyan Kesteloot. We have chosen to begin our

Originally published as 'Négritude césairienne, Négritude senghorienne' in *Revue de littérature comparée* 48(3–4) (July–December 1974): 409–19.

study from the moment when the neologism Negritude was coined, when Césaire and Senghor were still students. In 'Problématique de la negritude' (1971), the president-poet is eager to defend the purity of the term's grammatical formation: 'I refer you to Maurice Grévisse's French grammar titled *Le Bon Usage* and to the two studies by the University at Strasbourg devoted to the suffixes *ité* (from the Latin *itas*) and *itude* (from the Latin *itudo*) communicated to me by my friend Professor Robert Schilling.'[1] Is this really a matter for concern? The value of a word resides in its power of expression, in its capacity to awaken the required references in the intelligence and sensitivity of those who pronounce it and those who hear it. Even if Césaire had tortured all the rules of French grammar to coin this unusual word, no one would have thought of criticizing him since it had such an extraordinary impact.

Notebook of a Return to My Native Land represents an apogee in Césaire's work, equalled only by his *And the Dogs Were Silent* ([1956] 1990).[2] It is the *Notebook* that contains the famous cry passionately taken up by an entire generation:

My negritude is not a stone, its deafness hurled
against the clamour of the day
My negritude is not an opaque spot of dead water
over the dead eye of the earth
My negritude is neither a tower nor a cathedral

1 Léopold Sédar Senghor, 'Problematique de la Négritude' in *Présence africaine: revue culturelle du monde noir* 78 (1971): 3–26. Also available in Léopold Sédar Senghor, *Liberté, III: Négritude et civilisation de l'universel* (Paris: Seuil, 1977), pp. 268–89; here, p. 269.

2 Aimé Césaire, *And the Dogs Were Silent* in *Aimé Césaire: Lyric and Dramatic Poetry 1946–1982* (Clayton Eshlemann and Annette Smith trans) (Charlottesville: University of Virginia Press, 1990), pp. 1–76.

It reaches deep down into the red flesh of the soil
It reaches deep down into the blazing flesh of the
   sky
It pierces opaque prostration with its straight
   patience.[3]

The well-known itinerary that the *Notebook* traces is that of a young intellectual returning to the Antilles only to rediscover, at the end of his journey, not the paradise islands which two generations of would-be poets have described in a servile imitation of their French masters, such as Dominique Guesde:

> On the horizon, the sea and white cliff of
> Le Gosier; to the left with its green islets
> Where the swell of the ocean unfurls in rims of
>   foam
> On an azure bay where the north wind subsides
> Pointe-à-Pitre in the midst of its marshlands
> Spreads its Creole nonchalance and its French grace.[4]

Nor the isles of Saint-John Perse, the lost paradise of a young aristocrat's childhood: 'My nurse was a mestizo and smelled of the castor bean; always I noticed there were pearls of glistening sweat on her forehead, and around her eyes—and so warm, her mouth had the taste of rose-apples, in the river, before noon.'[5]

---

3 Césaire, *Notebook*, p. 115.

4 Dominique Guesde, 'Le Tray' [1897] in Jack Corzani (ed.), *Encyclopédie antillaise, 1: Poètes des Antilles-Guyane françaises* (Fort-de-France: Desormeaux, 1971), pp. 98–182; here, p. 98.

5 Saint-John Perse, 'To Celebrate a Childhood' (1907) in *Éloges and Other Poems*, bilingual edn (Louis Varèse trans.) (New York: Random House, Bollingen Series 55, 1956), pp. 6–22; here, p. 15.

But the Antilles is full of ugliness, misery and despair. Landing on his island, in his 'inert' town, the memory of his childhood comes back to him. The young intellectual sees himself as the 'somnolent little nigger' with the small joys of Christmas, for example, where 'there is black pudding, some two fingers thick, coiling like volubles, some broad and squat, the milder kind tasting like wild thyme, the more violent one spiced to incandescence.'[6]

He sees again his family, of modest origins, for he is a man of the people, his house, his street, his neighbourhood. But far from distancing himself with contempt or disgust from these 'death-bearers who turn in circles in this calabash of an island',[7] he draws closer to them and claims them as his own for he knows the long and painful path which has made them what they are and led them to where they are today. He therefore assumes responsibility for this people and consequently, for the entire black race. Their vices, their insanity, their wounds and suffering become his. Then, not content with assuming them, he magnifies them, he glorifies them, he turns them into virtues and claims to fame, adding pell-mell to the guilt of his individual meanness the major crimes attributed to his people and his race until the magnificent, ambiguous cry:

> Those who have invented neither gunpowder
>   nor the compass
> Those who have never known how to subdue
>   either steam or electricity
> Those who have explored neither the seas nor
>   the sky.[8]

6 Césaire, *Notebook*, p. 81.

7 Ibid., p. 89.

8 Ibid., p. 111.

We say 'ambiguous' because for Jean-Paul Sartre it is 'a lofty claim for the non-technical' whereas for Lilyan Kesteloot it is the objective, humble and saddened recognition of a *real* inferiority along with all the rest of the race's weak points.[9]

At the heart of the poem, the real problem is that of a lost identity that has been denied, recovered and forged at all costs and at any cost:

> I accept . . . I accept . . . completely, with no
>   reservation . . .
> My race which no ablution of hyssop mixed with
>   lilies
> could purify.
> my race blemished with maculas
> my race ripe grapes for drunken feet
> my queen of spit and leprosies.[10]

Here we come up against what appears to me to be the *Notebook's* great weakness. Through a transmutation whose alchemy is not revealed, the poet and his people, whose state of extreme humiliation has been described to us in great length, suddenly find themselves transformed:

> Negridom is standing
>
> sitting-down negridom
> unforeseenly standing
> standing in the hold

9 Jean-Paul Sartre, 'Black Orpheus' (1948) in *The Aftermath of War* (Chris Turner trans.) (Calcutta: Seagull Books, 2008), pp. 257–330, here, p. 300 (translation modified); Lilyan Kesteloot, *Les écrivains noirs de langue française: naissance d'une literature* (Brusells: Université libre de Bruxelles, 1983).

10 Césaire, *Notebook*, p. 121.

> standing in the cabins
> standing on deck
> standing in the wind
> standing under the sun
> standing in the blood
> standing
> > and
> > free[11]

Although for Kesteloot everything is clear, since the total identification of the poet with his people makes for *a miracle*, we, ourselves, reserve the right to refuse this miracle and would like to understand the logic behind it.[12] A voice, Césaire tells us, pierces 'the night and the audience like the penetrance of an apocalyptic wasp' and it 'pronounces that Europe has been stuffing us with lies and bloating us with pestilence for centuries'.[13] What is this voice? And where does it come from? What sudden about-turn makes this 'walking manure a hideous forerunner of tender cane and silky cotton' into a mass of men ripe for a victorious struggle?[14]

It would be easy to let oneself be carried away by the emotional magic of the *Notebook* if it was meant to be nothing more than a song, a political poem, a militant poem engaged in combat. It was no coincidence that on returning to his island the poet refused to be ensnared by the trap of exoticism. The Antilles, which for him emerged from 'the mud of the bay', have been fabricated by three

11 Ibid., p. 131.

12 Kesteloot, *Les écrivains noirs de langue française*

13 Césaire, *Notebook*, p. 125.

14 Ibid., p. 105.

centuries of colonial exploitation.[15] It was no coincidence that the crowd was 'strangely chattering and dumb', because it could only express itself with borrowed words.[16] The wounds were those inflicted on millions of black people taken into slavery. Those vices assumed as virtues are those Europe branded on them. Lastly, the refusal, whereby identity is forged, is the refusal of assimilation presented to the colonized subject as the only way to access the status of man and which silences the language of revolt from a people. In my opinion, the refusal to assimilate does not necessarily result in a struggle and can be based on a mistaken awareness that is even more harmful. Throughout the *Notebook,* what is Césaire asking of himself, and through him, asking of his people and his race? A total acceptance of the self as a Negro. But the Negro doesn't exist. Anxious to legitimize his exploitation, Europe completely fabricated him out of what it thought it possessed as well as what it knew was missing. Although it refused him intelligence, reason and beauty which it considered it possessed, it attributed to him brute, almost bestial, force and sexual enormity. In the myth of the Negro, this last attribution is the most interesting and clearly indicates how Europe felt itself cramped in the straitjacket of its morality and harked back to its licentiousness before the Middle Ages and Christianity. In order to arrive at the only stage that permits liberation, we have to stop thinking of ourselves as Negro. We have to dismantle the mechanism of exploitation which allows the propagation of such lies. We have to see ourselves as Man. Césaire, certainly conscious of this, hastily writes in his *Notebook*:

15 Ibid., p. 73.
16 Ibid., p. 75.

The old negritude
is gradually cadaverising
the horizon breaks, moves farther away and
expands
and through the tearing of clouds the dazzling of
a sign[17]

But we are by no means convinced. It seems simply to us that Negritude will undergo another metamorphosis and that we will go on being Negroes.

It can be said that in Césaire's time of outright assimilation what mattered was to refuse Europe's culture and its accompanying domination blindly and out of hand. We might ask, all things considered, whether there was refusal. Since it was Europe which fabricated the Negro, to claim this myth as one's true identity—or worse, glory in it—amounts to accepting Europe in its culture's worst erring ways. It means barricading oneself joyously and of one's free will in a ghetto which has been built as a trap and to set oneself up as a combatant. If individually the poet manages by way of a miracle to become aware of the mystifications of which he has been victim, will it be the same for the debased and degraded multitudes round him? Does he believe that his passion as leader will be enough?

Negritude takes a lie as a basic premise, the worst lie of colonization, the acceptance of an inferior being made for subaltern functions. Even a temporary recognition of this lie seems to me eminently dangerous. And since in the end this lie is exposed, be it a little too quickly, in Césaire's *Notebook*, acceptance is useless. The main refusal must be of the word Negro and its related loathsome mythology. To revel in the memory of suffering and humiliation

17 Ibid., p. 129.

inflicted on our race amounts to a dubious masochism from which nothing constructive can come about. If *Notebook of a Return to My Native Land* is said to be a descent into hell, it is not only a sublime descent but also somewhat gratuitous. The suffering and humiliation are nothing. Understanding the conditions which fuelled them and kept them alive is all that matters. This alone can give them their true meaning.

Theoretically, President Senghor's Negritude takes over from the first, the one he helped forge with Césaire. It corresponds to the stage where the Negro, now free, 'stands tall' to build his Civilization. As we have said, it is meant to be an ideology for the Black World. It is not my purpose here to join in the chorus of critics such as Wole Soyinka, Marcien Towa, Stanislas Adotevi, Yves Benot and René Depestre who in varying degrees have attacked it and attempted to prove that it merely sanctions a dichotomy of the world which gives to the Negro peoples a series of spiritual gifts, such as 'a sense of community, a sense of hierarchy, a sense of the divine, a sense of an art which plunges its roots into life which is as much and even more an exercise of the soul as it is of the mind'[18] and gives to Europe, and more generally to the White World, the material profit that its technical genius deserves. We shall merely indicate how the seeds of weakness begin to appear openly in Senghor's poetry.

Senghor has had no experience of Césaire's powerful masochism. Not simply because Césaire is an Antillean, i.e. a direct descendant of a transplanted slave, and Senghor

18 Léopold Sédar Senghor, 'Vues sur l'Afrique noire ou assimiler, non être assimilés' in *Liberté, I: Négritude et Humanisme* (Paris: Seuil, 1964), p. 68.

an African, not removed from his roots, but more because one is a child of the people and the other, the son of opulent landowners (he never lets us forget it) who therefore belongs to that category of African society which, although it did not directly collaborate with European capitalism in exploiting the masses (we are thinking of those feudal African chiefs and dignitaries trafficking in the rewards of the slave trade as well as the new traditional chiefs artificially consolidated by Europe as docile instruments of its domination) did see its privileges relatively respected by the colonizers. This quotation from 'Problématique de la negritude' provides the key to Senghor's Africa: 'When I read the first pages of *Origin of African Cultures* by Leo Frobenius I relived my strict childhood in the kingdom of Sine, even though it was then reduced to a protectorate. I remembered, among other scenes, the visit by King Koumba Ndofène to my father, where every feeling was noble, every manner courteous and every word beautiful.'

He is thinking of this Africa of chiefs in sumptuous robes with their griots, their warriors, their herds of cattle, their *koras* and their slaves. And if later he claims to rip the 'Banania grin from all the walls of France', it is because he is protesting a mask which disfigures the *beauty* of his African idol.[19] Let us open haphazardly a collection of poems by Senghor. The accents of revolt are few and far between. In *Hosties noires* (1948, Black Hosts), let us read the poem dedicated to the Senegalese infantrymen who died for France:

19 Léopold Sédar Senghor, 'Poème liminaire' (1940) in *Oeuvre poétique* (Paris: Seuil, 1990), p. 57. Available in English as 'Preliminary Poem' in *Léopold Sédar Senghor, The Collected Poetry* (Melvin Dixon trans. and introd.) (Charlottesville: University of Virginia Press, 1991), p. 309 (translation modified).

Listen to us, corpses lying in the water deep in the
northern and eastern plains

Receive this red earth under the summer sun red-
dened by the blood of the white hosts

Receive the greetings from your black comrades,
Senegalese infantrymen

WHO DIED FOR THE REPUBLIC![20]

No questioning of why they died. No protest about
using these black forces in a slaughter that didn't concern
them. On the contrary, in the 'Prayer of the Tirailleur
Sénégalais' (1938), the cry goes up to the Lord: 'We offer
You our bodies together with those of the French peasants,
our comrades.'[21]

Although in the course of combat the poet meets
black American soldiers, men who have strayed like him
into defending a White World which has always refused
them the status of man, it is certainly not to encourage
them to withdraw from combat, like the black militants in
Vietnam today, but to call themselves 'Afrika!' before they
recover the lost laughter and greet the ancient voice and
roar of the Congo's cascades. In a word, it is to engage in
an emotional and racial recognition which leads to nothing. The only poem where there are precise accusations
against colonization is 'Prayer for Peace' (1945) where for-
giveness immediately obliterates any scathing note the
attacks may possess. And, above all, it is obvious that Senghor distinguishes between two Frances:

20 Léopold Sédar Senghor, 'Aux Tirailleurs Sénégalais morts pour la
France' in *Oeuvre poétique*, pp. 65–7; 'Prayer of the Tirailleur Sénégalais' in *Collected Poetry*, p. 322 (translation modified).

21 Ibid.

> Oh Lord, banish from my memory the France
> which is not France, this mask of pettiness and
> hate on the face of France.

> This mask of pettiness and hate for which I have
> only hatred.[22]

And there we have it, the exploitation, exactions, abuse of all sorts and violence is attributed to the bad side of France. The world is full of 'traitors and imbeciles'. The true France, ah, the true France is the one which 'from one day to the next turned slaves into men freely, equally and fraternally' (Senghor is unaware of the powerful economic reason behind the abolition of slavery) and demands a place for France 'at the right hand of the Father'. And it is not only with respect to Europe that the poet demonstrates this surprising indulgence. Confronted with America and the terrible problem of exploitation and racism, he merely exclaims:

> New York! New York, let the black blood flow
> Into your blood
> Let it oil the rust from your steel articulations
> Let it give your bridges the curve of a rump and
> the suppleness of lianas.[23]

And here we have arrived at the famous dichotomy: the Negro giving the West, atrophied by the excesses of its technical genius, a vague spiritual wealth. What is Senghor's Negritude content with? With glorifying an Africa

22 Léopold Sédar Senghor, 'Prière de Paix' in *Oeuvre poétique*, pp. 92–8; 'Prayer for Peace' in *Collected Poetry*, pp. 69–72 (translation modified).

23 Léopold Sédar Senghor, 'A New York' in *Éthiopiques* (Paris: Presence Africaine, 1956), p. 116; 'New York' in *Collected Poetry*, pp. 87–9; here, p. 88 (translation modified).

extinct, the Africa of the great empires buried in dust. With a reminder of a long-defunct way of life. A biblical and epic incantation whereby exercising the names of people ('Dyôb! I told him, Belaup of Kaymôr!' Or names of places: 'Dyôb! From Ngabôu to Walo, from Ngalam to the sea')[24] or alliteration, assonance, inversion and all the subtleties of a perfectly controlled style help resurrect the antique soul of noble Africa:

> Furnishings from Guinea and Congo, heavy and polished, somber and serene
> Masks primordial and pure on the walls, remote yet so present!
> Stools of honor for the hereditary hosts, for the princes of the Upper Country.
> Musky perfumes, thick mats of silence
> Cushions of shade and leisure, the sound of a fountain of peace.
> Elegant words.[25]

The intention, of course, is clear. Give to every Negro, crushed by the belief in the inferiority of his race, the pride of belonging to a world that built wisdom, beauty and knowledge. We doubt, however, whether the immigrant worker, the inhabitant of the slums round the new African capitals and the unemployed are likely to be convinced by such language. Even more seriously, we wonder whether Senghor's vision of ancient Africa resists the expert eye of the researcher. Ancient Africa had its flaws as well as its virtues. To dwell at length on the latter and systematically

24 Léopold Sédar Senghor, 'Taga de Mbaye Diop' in *Hosties Noires*, p. 80. See 'Taga For Mbaye Dyob' in *Collected Poetry*, pp. 55–6.

25 Léopold Sédar Senghor, 'And We Shall Be Steeped' in *Collected Poetry*.

relegate the former to obscurity is to lapse into exaggeration which might very well miss its objective. What flaws, wonders the Negro, did this highly praised Africa consist of to make the scaffolding of its civilization collapse so entirely? What internal weakness, what shortcomings, what failings? Was it possible that the enemy was so formidable? And then its power and skill at making us what we are, shouldn't we in our actual destitute state admire it and even imitate it? A path wide open to this assimilation which Senghor claims to revolt against.

Nigerian historian Onwuka Dike writes that we must assume our past such as it is—the splendours of the art of Benin as well as the horrors of human sacrifice. And Europe too must assume its past—the masterpieces by El Greco as well as the horrors of the Inquisition.[26] This statement seems to me to be the best refutation of Negritude we could possibly have. Listen to Sartre explain to us the scope and effectiveness of Negritude: 'Since he is oppressed in his race and because of it, the Negro must first of all be made aware of his race.'[27] It is absurd, however, to claim that the Negro has been oppressed *because of his race*. During the fifteenth, sixteenth and seventeenth centuries, African peoples were exploited with the complicity of their chiefs to such a degree that, it must be said in their defence, the chiefs had not foreseen. The large-scale slavery they practised in their various kingdoms paved the way for the transatlantic slave trade with all its horrors and degradation. The suffering endured by this transplantation, how-

26 See Onwuka Dike, *Trade and Politics in the Niger Delta, 1830–1885: An Introduction to the Economic and Political History of Nigeria* (Oxford: Clarendon Press, 1956).

27 Sartre, 'Black Orpheus', *The Aftermath of War*, p. 268 (translation modified).

ever, did not affect the different categories of African society in the same way, even though, in the end, it shook every one of them to the core. Whereas the future slaves or pieces of eight swallowed their tongues and tried to die in the holds of the slave ships, the kings of Bonny, Calabar, Dahomey, Ardres and Jolof (the list would be too long to mention here) climbed on board those very same ships to drink brandy with the English, French and Portuguese officers and receive payment for their human cargo. Although, from the very beginnings of imperialism, African societies were increasingly dependent on and subjected to the West, this was never done without the conscious agreement of the so-called elites and minority who profited from Europe and, to a lesser degree, from the subjection of their peoples. The kings of Bonny, Calabar, Dahomey, Ardres and Jolof were black. Like the heads of state received today in great pomp by the European capitals. Like those who died in Aubervilliers.

You will say we are a long way from literature. Not so. Since Negritude is not meant to be simply an inspiration for melodious songs. In the case of Césaire, it is supposed to be a prior, temporary but vital, awareness which leads to the fight for freedom. In the case of Senghor, a recognition of the Black World's cultural values and hence, a source of strength, pride and exhilaration faced with the desiccative technical nature of the White World. For me, it is a sentimental and futile trap. Taking as its foundation an illusory 'racial' community founded on a legacy of suffering, it obliterates the real problems which have always been of a political, social and economic nature. We are neither a race of subhumans nor of martyrs. We have not suffered passively an odious fate. We have helped forge it through the greed, selfishness and blindness of our leaders and the little concern we have for our masses.

Let us thank Negritude, however, for giving us the *Notebook of a Return to My Native Land*, perhaps the most beautiful poem written by a colonized subject.

> Blood! Blood! all our blood moved by the male
>   heart of the sun
> those who know the feminity of oil-bodied moon
>   the reconciled
> rapture of the antelope and the star
> those whose survival moves in the germination
>   of grass!
> Eia perfect circle of the world and closed
>   concordance![28]

Then let us relegate it to the rank of non-essential props of an obsolete melodrama. Our liberation goes through knowing that there have never been Negroes— that there have only ever been exploited men. Through understanding lucidly and serenely the causes, conditions and consequences of this exploitation.

28 Césaire, *Notebook*, p. 115.

Why Negritude?
Negritude or Revolution?

At the conference on Negritude in Dakar from 12 to 18 April, under the auspices of the Senegalese Progressive Union, poet Lèon-Gontran Damas exclaimed: 'In my opinion and whatever they may say, we are currently witnessing the triumph of Negritude (such as I see it anyway).' Struck by these words and keen to share their enthusiasm, I in turn looked at the state of the Black World over the years 1970–71. Oddly enough, 1970 began with a drama that made headlines in the press: the death in January of five immigrant workers, two Mauritanians and three Senegalese, in a slum in Aubervilliers.

Beyond the death of these five Africans there emerges the whole issue of immigrant workers whose plight France shares with the UK and the USA. The figures speak for themselves: 300,000 coloured immigrant workers in France, mostly Senegalese; 450,000 in the UK, mostly West Indian; and almost 500,000 Haitian immigrants in the USA and

Originally published as 'Pourquoi la négritude? Négritude ou revolution?' in Jeanne Lydie-Goré (ed.), *Négritude Africaine, Négritude Caraïbe* (Paris: Université de Paris-Nord, Centre d'Études Francophones: Éditions de la Francité, 1973), pp. 150–4. Proceedings of the conference 'African Negritude, Caribbean Negritude', organized by Jeanne-Lydie Gorée at Paris-Nord, Villetaneuse.

Canada.[1] These men and women belong to independent countries and are no longer the unwilling subjects of European nations.

Let us continue our survey where I can list haphazardly in the USA the indictment of nine members of the Black Panthers following a police raid on an apartment in Chicago, which was supposed to be the movement's headquarters, during which two men were shot in cold blood.[2] In Georgia, the governor, Lester Maddox, calls out the National Guard and 50 police officers to restore order following a race riot, resulting in six dead, all blacks of course, and 60 wounded.[3] In Mississippi, two students were gunned down by the police; and in Hartford, a young black minister, Ralph Abernathy, called for a march to protest the growing repression against blacks in the USA.[4] In Rhodesia, Leopold Takawira, former leader of the Zimbabwe African National Union, died [in 1970] from torture in Salisbury where he had been imprisoned since 1964. In England, Mr Heath's government decided to sell arms to South Africa despite verbal protests from 35 African countries represented at the UN. In Guadeloupe, there were massive strikes [1965–67] by farm workers, labourers and students; and off the coast of Africa, 18 black sailors were discovered in horrendous conditions on board a Norwegian vessel, registered in Liberia, forced to work 20 hours a day and beaten with iron bars and chains by a white crew.

I could go on much longer. I haven't even mentioned the wars in Angola, Mozambique and Guinea-Bissau.

1 *Le Journal Officiel*, 1970.

2 *Le Journal Officiel*, May 1969.

3 *Le Journal Officiel*, May 1970.

4 *Le Journal Officiel*, May 1968.

I simply want to say that I have difficulty seeing what motivated Mr Damas' enthusiasm given the state of the Black World and I am more inclined to think along the lines of Eldridge Cleaver who from Hanoi denounced the growing repression of black people in the USA and round the world.

Have I rightly understood the meaning of the terms used by Mr Damas, in particular the term Negritude? In order to help me in my quest, I refer to the advice from Mr Piquion, representing the Duvalier government at this same conference: 'In order to understand Negritude we have to make an effort to remember and relive the horrors of slavery, the pain of colonization and the humiliation of discrimination.'

I therefore turned my attention to the period of the Atlantic slave trade. In the light of recent studies, it appears evident that this slave trade could not have started, developed, and even existed, without the agreement and active participation of the Africans themselves. Let us recall certain facts. The slave trade was commerce, and commerce means two parties. There was nothing disorganized or anarchic about it. The parties to the slave trade were the traditional African chiefs, represented by their trafficking dignitaries (in the words of Basil Davidson)[5] and the European merchant navigators. Precise rules were established. Throughout the history of the slave trade, only three protests by African kings have been recorded: around 1540, Mani Kongo, converted to Catholicism under the name of King Alfonso I, complained about the fate of his people and asked to be sent doctors, medication and schoolteachers

5 See Basil Davidson, *Black Mother: The Years of the African Slave Trade* (Boston, MA: Little Brown and Company, 1961).

instead of merchants. Around 1724, King Agada of Dahomey sent a letter of protest to the British government. In 1789, Almamy of Fouta Toro complained to the French. As a rule, though, the African kings were very cooperative. They even asked the Europeans to help them in their domestic quarrels. In 1480, the king of the Jolofs, victim of a *coup d'état*, took refuge in a Portuguese fort, then fled to Lisbon where he hoped to obtain reinforcements. Around 1567, King of Sierra Leone and King Castro, confronted with a common enemy, called upon the services of the famous English slave trader, Hawkins, to come to their aid. In exchange for his services, John Hawkins received 470 captives. Damel of Cayor went even further and assumed the right to sell his own subjects.

I took a certain pleasure in noting the list, drawn up by Pierre Verger, of some of the presents the African and European sovereigns gave to one another.

> In 1728, Agada, King of Dahomey, sent a dwarf to the king of Portugal in exchange for a parasol.
>
> In 1750, Tegbessou sent Lisbon three negresses and a bundle of cloth wrappers from the Mina coast. The three women were employed in the queen's bedchamber. In exchange, Tegbessou received a dressing gown and a bonnet. When he complained it was not enough, he was sent a sedan chair and portable organ.
>
> In 1797, Abandozan sent the king of Portugal two cloth wrappers, four elephant tusks and two very lovely negresses; in exchange, he requested 300 barrels of gunpowder, pieces of silk, guns, parasols and bottles for storing his brandy and offered to complete his dispatch with several

handsome slaves if they found his request too expensive.[6]

I shall not persevere any further. It is obvious, therefore, that the slave trade was the result of collusion between black and white sovereigns whose common concern was profit, to the detriment of their people. Consequently, the bastion on which Mr Piquion claimed to base his understanding of Negritude cracks and falters. Although, subsequently, African society did slide into a relationship of dependence with Europe, and, if in the struggle between the ruling classes of Europe and the ruling classes of Africa, the latter emerged defeated, (a double misfortune for their people who had already suffered enough), both ruling classes were responsible for the suffering of the black masses up to the nineteenth century. The traditional African chiefs protested when the English —for economic reasons and not humanitarian, need we say—abolished the slave trade!

New World societies were formed on the basis of slavery, although even here it was not a factor of unity since very soon there emerged the free man of colour, the house slave and beneath them the field slave who formed the castes that would constitute the future classes. But to make it out to be the basis of unity of the black race, founded on a community of suffering, is not only to go against historical truth but also to be victim of the generalizations by Europe who, with the expansion of the slave trade, took black to mean slave and forgot all knowledge of the powerful African kingdoms existing in the fifteenth, sixteenth and seventeenth centuries.

6 See Pierre Verger, *Flux et Reflux de la Traite des Nègres entre le Golfe de Benin et Bahia de Todos Os Santos du XVIIe au XIXe siècle* (Paris: Mouton, 1968).

In my predicament, therefore, for the understanding of Negritude, I thought it best to turn to a country where Negritude was at work, to Haiti where 'negritude stood up for the first time.'[7] So I consulted Haiti's statistics:

Infant mortality rate: 17.2 per cent

Life expectancy at birth: 32 years

Literacy rate: 10.5 per cent (the lowest in Latin America)

Children in primary education: 24 per cent

Children in secondary education: 1.7 per cent

Medical care: one doctor per 15,000 inhabitants

National income per head: US$ 80 (the lowest in Latin America)

Gross Domestic Product: US$ 86.[8]

These figures, René Depestre tells us, indicate a neo-colony at the rock bottom of its socioeconomic and socio-cultural crisis.

Is this where we land up then when Negritude stands tall? I had preferred to think Duvalier a horrible accident of history, a loathsome avatar. And I worked back to the founding of the republic when Santo Domingo became Haiti. Haitian independence was won, we know, at the price of a bloody struggle (1791–1804). We also know the fundamental role played by the slaves. But it is worthwhile pointing out a few facts. Before the war of liberation, the characteristic of Santo Domingo was the concentration of land ownership in just a few hands. A minority of white planters owned about 8,000 plantations on the island. Some of them were so vast that they stretched 4.5 or 10

7 Césaire, *Notebook*, p. 91.

8 Conseil National de la Statistique et de l'Informatique, 1970.

leagues long as well as wide. The large plantation, therefore, was typically managing hundreds of slaves.

Besides these wealthy planters, a new land-owning class emerged—the free men of colour, mulattoes and Negroes, who owned a third of the plantations in Santo Domingo and a quarter of the slaves. What happened when Louverture came to power? The constitution he established in 1801 ratified the principle of the large plantation since it prohibited dividing up domains smaller than 50 hectares. Since the white planters had fled in terror, the freed Negroes and mulattoes settled on the vacant land and took possession. The former slaves, now theoretically free peasants, were subjected to a system of forced labour from six in the morning to five in the afternoon but given no right to ownership of the land where they worked. The former class of free Negroes and mulattoes swelled the ranks of the revolutionary army as generals to whom Louverture distributed land. Dessalines consequently cried out: 'We have waged war for the others.'[9] And Louverture fell into the trap laid by the French. Once Dessalines took over power, he nationalized the white planters' assets, created the Administration of State Domains for controlling the development of the plantations, for conducting a new economic policy and, consequently, for putting the revolution to work.

We know the fate that awaited him—he was assassinated in 1806 by a coalition of wealthy Negroes and mulattoes. Alexandre Pétion and Henri Christophe who succeeded him gave in to the demands of this class of nouveaux riches and sold off the domains nationalized by Dessalines. And what

9 See Justin Chrysostome Dorsainvil, *Manuel d'histoire d'Haiti* (Port-au-Prince: Henri Duchamp, 1934).

about the masses, the people? According to Jean Price-Mars, the change was more apparent than real, superficial rather than deep, and occurred in a slippage of political power from the hands of the white aristocracy—it was nothing more than a substitution of masters. The white planters were dispossessed by the black and mulatto leaders who then claimed the very same privileges and prerogatives. The larger mass of people remained confined to the job of producing without tools or technical knowledge.[10]

By this all too rapid incursion into an area far removed from literature, I have tried to show that, from the very start, our peoples have been divided into two groups of identical colour: the exploiters, and the exploited. Those such as Queen Tétou, Tegbessou and Agada who sell and grow rich. Those who are sold and swallow their tongues in the holds of the slave ships; those who, despite their country gaining independence, continue to migrate and die in the slums of Europe; and those who are received in great pomp by the capitals of this very same Europe and lecture on the black's sense of rhythm. The exploiters have never taken into consideration the colour of the exploited. They have let themselves be manoeuvred by the Portuguese, French, English and Americans when it blindly and selfishly served their class interests. The exploiters have no colour, and the masses of the New World in Brazil, Jamaica, Cuba, Martinique and Guadeloupe have a proverb for it: 'Nèg' qui ni l'agent, pas nèg' enco' (A Negro who has money is no longer a Negro).

And in this world divided from the very beginning by a deep division between the classes, here they talk of

10 See Jean Price-Mars, *Ainsi parla l'oncle* (Montreal: Mémoire d'Encrier, 2009).

Negritude! They talk of a unity of the Black World based on a community of suffering which is said to have been inflicted on the entire race. Worse, they tell me that only racial awareness can liberate this world, a precondition for progress.

'And since he is oppressed in his race and because of it, it is first of his race that it is necessary for him to take conscience. He must compel those, who, during the centuries, have vainly attempted, because he was a Negro, to reduce him to the status of the beast, to recognize him as a man.' Thus speaks Sartre in 'Black Orpheus'.[11] It is an unfortunate simplification of history. The Negro has not been exploited because of his race. Colette Guillaumin, like several sociologists before her, recalls that the justification for exploiting the black peoples for their so-called racial inferiority is relatively recent—the myth of the Negro, as it is called, was born around the middle of the nineteenth century.[12] It would, indeed, be interesting to study this myth in the light of Europe's frustrated shortcomings.

The justification by racial inferiority is the most recent form of a series of justifications. The first were social and geographic—it was said that the African who was taken to the Americas found the climate, the habitat and the way of life the same as those back home. One of the pretexts was the existence of slavery in traditional African societies—even though it was different in nature—and the fact that all these men and women were sold by the African chiefs themselves.

11 Sartre, 'Black Orpheus' in *The Aftermath of War*, p. 268 (translation modified).

12 See Colette Guillaumin, *Racism, Sexism, Power and Ideology* (London: Routledge, 1995).

There was also the religious justification—the Africans didn't believe in the true God. This was, we are told, the argument that led Louis XIII to contract *asientos* with Spain. This very Christian king refused to conduct the commerce of men and he had to be persuaded that they were making Christians out of the slaves. He believed them.

The justification for the exploitation of the so-called racial inferiority occurred when the slave trade had taken on enormous proportions and when the image of the Negro as beast of burden in the plantations of the New World was already widespread. It asserted itself when Europe was preparing to switch from the colonial trading posts and establishments to the systematic exploitation of African territories. It corresponded with a new turning point in European scientific thought. In short, race is but the last cloak thrown on the exploitation of the African peoples.

I have been told there are two Negritudes. Even if it is not expressed as frankly as I am about to, it is acknowledged, mostly by young people, that there is a 'good Negritude', Césaire's, and a 'bad Negritude', Senghor's. Why differentiate between the two? On analysing the Césaire's *Notebook*, it appears that his Negritude is a movement in double time.

> Césaire is conscious of his people's despair
>
> He assumes it, becomes its bard and herald
>
> Beyond his fellow Antillians, he assumes his entire race.

Then, explains Kesteloot, Césaire's total identification with his people produces a miracle: 'And suddenly, strength and life charge at me like a bull and the tide of life surrounds the taste bud of the morne.'[13]

Allow me not to believe in miracles. How can the total identification with an object of contempt, with a schizophrenic being, steel one for liberation and combat? The response will be that it is a question of refusing, refusing cultural assimilation, among others—anything, rather than continue wanting to be white. But what refusal are we talking about? Since it is Europe which fabricated the Negro myth, doesn't the fact of assuming this myth and glorying in it as an expression of one's true personality amount to accepting Europe and its culture in its worst erring ways? Refusal? I find it hard to believe that there is a refusal here. I see nothing but total acceptance. Yet a few lines later, Césaire denounces the myth he previously assumed: 'Europe has been stuffing us with lies and bloating us with pestilence for centuries.'[14]

I am trying hard not to be surprised at this abrupt about-turn. I won't insist on a rational explanation. But I do ask: Why did he have to revel in a so-called racial abjection if later he was to denounce it? What do we gain by this? Couldn't we spare ourselves this contradiction? The logical step would have been to demonstrate from the very beginning the falsehood of the Negro myth and expose the exploitation that it claims to justify.

Continuing my reading of the *Notebook*, I come across the lines:

13 See Barthelemy Kotchy, with Lilyan Kesteloot, *Aimé Césaire, l'homme et l'oeuvre* (Paris: Presence Africaine, 1993); Césaire, *Notebook*, p. 125.

14 Césaire, *Notebook*, p. 125.

I cry hurrah!
The old negritude
is gradually cadaverising,
the horizon breaks, moves farther away and expands.[15]

Must I conclude that Césaire predicts a future Negritude? Allow me to be concerned about the promise of an eternal future for the Negro, even though I have not been told of the shape my new Negritude will take. And in my eyes it is in the prolongation of this ambiguity that Senghor's Negritude falls into place, which is nothing more than the application on a political, social and economic level of the Negritude he conceived with Césaire. At a time when Césaire expressed his Negritude in a powerful masochism whose beauty we do not contest but rather its usefulness, Senghor revived what Césaire, descendant of the slaves of the New World, was hardly authorized to do—relive the splendour of an Africa still alive in the memory of his elders, the Africa of traditional chiefs and noble warriors.

The rediscovery of the African past and the assertion that the African continent had a history was certainly useful, could even be taken seriously and pass for revolutionary since Senghor was attributed the epithet of politically committed. We are thus faced with a movement with two versions: an African version where the bard of those who remained on the continent recalls a lost grandeur; and a Caribbean version where the bard of those who had been transplanted and lost everything, after having revelled in their abjection, endeavours to cling to the glory of his distant ancestors, those who in fact had sold him.

In 1946, however—contradiction of contradictions—Césaire urged the people of the French Antilles to vote for

15 Ibid., p. 129.

assimilation, in favour of an overseas department status for Martinique and Guadeloupe, and in 1958 he reiterated his attachment to the Fifth Republic. In other words, Negritude did not even have time to stand tall in both islands as it was supposed to have done in Haiti. It was the victim of infanticide and was stillborn. And let us rejoice when we see what happens when it comes to power as in Senegal. That's where it reveals its true face. It is content with the so-called recognition of Africa's dignity by Europe. It sanctions the dichotomy of the world—Europe's apparent desiccation from technology and Africa's wealth of spiritual values.

What does the so-called recognition by Europe mean if it doesn't come with material and economic improvements for the African masses? What but a dangerous trap? What but an attempt at diversion in order to operate on the quiet, while the people engage in the so-called traditional songs and dances? I would like to recall Nkrumah for whom the main obstacle to African development was precisely that traditional society as it appears today—nothing more than an anachronistic parody of what it must have been in the past.

A new class of semi-privileged emerged alongside the old chiefdoms, the national bourgeoisie, which faithfully served the foreign capital from which it draws its very relative power. Need I quote Fanon?

> The national bourgeoisie discovers its historical mission as intermediary [. . .] its vocation is not to transform the nation but prosaically serve as a conveyor belt for capitalism, forced to camouflage itself behind the mask of neo-colonialism. The national bourgeoisie, with no misgivings and with

great pride, revels in the role of agent in its dealings with the Western bourgeoisie.[16]

And what about the people? The masses become impoverished. An urban sub-proletariat is created. A modern version of slaves, the immigrant workers come to empty Europe's garbage and incidentally die in Aubervilliers.

But what about culture, you will say, the culture which the advocates of Negritude have made their battle cry and Trojan horse? Forgive me for quoting Fanon again: 'To fight for national culture first of all means fighting for the liberation of the nation.'[17] And by liberation we do not mean substituting one form of exploitation for another.

Should we be surprised that Negritude in the hands of the powerful is so harmful when it relies on so much confusion? When it claims to divert the demands of the economically exploited in favour of racial recrimination? But what about racism, they'll say, since racism is Negritude's only justification? But what do I care if the West is victim to its own myths or perpetrates them? What matters to me is that I refuse to perpetrate them, that I refuse any label, any categorization which aims to restrict, orientate or channel the expression of my aspirations and demands, that I refuse to belong to a specific branch of the human species possessing a lot of this and a little of that. What matters is that I realize that my exploitation is but one of the many faces of exploitation which bombs Vietnam, supports military dictatorships in Latin America and prisons in Burgos.

16 Fanon, *The Wretched of the Earth*, pp. 100–1.
17 Ibid., p. 168.

Césaire's version of Negritude is nothing but a gratuitous descent into hell, a masochism with no effect on the struggle for liberation which it is supposed to achieve.

Liberation can only be achieved by the prior refusal of any racial stand and the prior assertion of our position in the family of man. As for Senghor's version of Negritude —since it operates on the political level, that is where we need to challenge it. But that is another story.

The Difficult Relationship with Africa

AN INTERVIEW WITH MARYSE CONDÉ

AUTREMENT. Having lived in Africa and written about the continent in *Segu*, you have made your own return to your native land, to the people who have invented nothing, to paraphrase Césaire. Do you feel you have landed on another planet or in terra incognita?

MARYSE CONDÉ. Perhaps I should rectify Césaire's words by saying that they were about a period when we did believe we had invented nothing, and that they are about not only the people of the Caribbean but the entire Black World. Ever since I have returned to the Caribbean, I have felt, on the contrary, that it is a place of great creativity. A place where a great many influences have met, where cultural elements from numerous origins have mixed, and that the Caribbean has indeed invented something, i.e. Caribbean culture, a culture which for a very long time it has ignored. Please don't ask me to define it because a culture cannot be defined, it is lived. It's the ethnologists, or rather the anthropologists, who lecture on the com-

Interview by Richard Philcox, husband and translator. Originally published as 'Le difficile rapport à l'Afrique' in Daniel Bastien and Maurice Lemoine (eds), *Antilles Espoirs et déchirements de l'âme créole* (Paris: Autrement, 1989), pp. 101–5.

ponents of a culture and define it. A people live their culture and are incapable of slicing it up like a sausage. Consequently, I see Caribbean culture being lived all round me but perhaps the people of the Caribbean, who possess it, don't always have the feeling that it is precious or valuable. Perhaps they doubt the validity of this culture and perhaps the role of the writer is to make them aware that what they carry in them is extremely dynamic and beautiful. So, I haven't landed on another planet; I've landed in a place where there is a hidden treasure, a kind of forest that has to be cleared.

AUTREMENT. Now that you have made this return, do you have any doubts about the validity of such a move?

MARYSE CONDÉ. Humans are tortured and changeable beings and I would be lying if I didn't say that there are moments when I wonder if I have made the right choice. Because Guadeloupe is an island, a kind of cocoon, womb and uterus in which you can easily fall asleep, especially when you are in my position, i.e. when you live in the country, in a nice house with fields and trees opposite and the mountains and sea on the horizon. One can shut oneself away in this cozy little universe and forget the real world, even the harsh reality of the island. So there are days when I feel somewhat drowsy, 'in a state of sleep' as they say in Guadeloupe. But it is only temporary and the next day I realize that a lot of things—too many things, perhaps—are calling me and I start over by trying to help with everything that is in gestation here.

AUTREMENT. Is it important for a writer to be at home or should a writer be constantly on the move like V. S. Naipaul?

MARYSE CONDÉ. I believe that even at home in Guadeloupe I am somewhat on the move because whenever I meet with Guadeloupeans—those who have never left the island—and talk to them, I realize there is a distance between them and me. The Guadeloupeans with whom I feel at harmony are those who, like me, have lived outside the island, and, to a certain extent, still think—and still dream—of the outside. In other words, you return home physically and settle in a place, your body is there but your head and your imagination continue to go back and forth between the places you have known and those you would like to know. I think that if the mind does not roam, there is no creativity. I don't think one can create in a status quo, in a kind of blind entrenchment. I believe you should wander. To roam is salutary. What I am trying to do today in my journey as a writer is to capture a Caribbean moment, to write a story which will be more Caribbean than the ones I have already written. But this does not mean that my next book and the one after will be the same. I believe that the act of writing is a sort of continuous movement, constantly changing, a kind of flowing water that is always starting afresh. It has all been said before me, hence literary creation is constantly starting over again. I don't believe in entrenchment—I believe in a physical return but the mind must continue to roam.

AUTREMENT. Does being in Guadeloupe mean 'writing differently'?

MARYSE CONDÉ. Yes, and this is a fundamental problem. Critics who analyse my style will see full well the difference between the novel I'm writing now and *Segu*.

In *Segu*, we followed the characters one after the other. There were descriptions of them and dialogue. The novelist was, so to speak, in the mind, the head and the heart of each of the characters; she made them act and brought them together. Whereas now I believe a Caribbean novel should have a narrator who is a little like the descendant of the traditional storyteller. He is the one who narrates the story. There can be dialogue but only very briefly. As a rule it is reported speech, things the narrator has heard and attempts to recreate. It is he, his gaze, which envelops the story, gives it a kind of circular shape and draws out, so to speak, its symbolism and meaning. Furthermore, the speech of the narrator, the heir to the traditional storyteller, is both epic, since the epic can be found in the people, and humoristic. Major events like deaths and births are always narrated with a touch of mockery. In *Tree of Life*, for example, there is a character who is a militant patriot for independence and who dies in a bomb explosion. The narrator introduces doubt about the very reason for his death by saying that he may have killed himself or had himself killed because of a woman. Hence the narrator resists the grandiloquence or hackneyed stereotypes of what we call high literature and instead endeavours to recreate that very important side, in my opinion, of Caribbean mentality—the cheeky humorous side. Even in the tensest situation, there is mockery. There is laughter. And laughter, in the end, has a very deep meaning.

AUTREMENT. When you write, do you take Creole into account? Do you think the Creole language adds something to the French language or, on the contrary, drags it down?

MARYSE CONDÉ. It's very complicated. My knowledge of
Creole is very limited. Many Antilleans who have lived
most of their life outside are like me and 'their' Creole
is very poor. Now I am in the process of learning Creole again, so to speak. I don't have a direct use for Creole when I write. I have rediscovered, rather, a kind of
French speech by Creolophones. I can remember the
environment in which I grew up. My parents and their
friends—although they did not speak Creole, the
French they spoke was in direct contact with Creole.
They said things like *I took to sleep* instead of *I fell asleep*,
I took a leap instead of *I fell*, etc. What I found fascinating was to reintroduce those Creolized French images
into my writing. I am not yet at the stage where I can
write directly in Creole. First of all, the people round
me who speak Creole speak it very badly. In order to
find a perfectly harmonious and poetic Creole, I
would need to consult the 'traditionalists'. Alain Rutil,
for example, has collected *The Wonderful Words of
Albert Gaspard* (1987).[1] I would need to find that sort
of Guadeloupean. I haven't found him yet! The people
I meet every day are perhaps politically motivated but
their Creole seems terrible to me. They take French
words, add a bit of spice here and there and make it
into a hybrid language. I would need to go to the
source, to the people who still possess this beautiful
language. I haven't yet done so. But I wonder: If I did,
would I be doing something useful or would I be like
the ethnologist who digs up the past or a grammarian
in search of obsolete expressions? Must we reinsert

1 Alain Rutil, *Les belles paroles d'Albert Gaspard* (Paris: Editions
caribéennes, 1987).

them at all cost into modern speech and writing as some are doing? We are in 1987 in Guadeloupe. Perhaps this speech, precious though it may be, belongs to a tradition which obviously should be revered but which is out of date. We should live with our times. We should look to the future. For better or for worse, Creole is infiltrated with French and that is its modern form. It is not necessarily a sign of its coming demise. It is perhaps merely a sign of the way it is developing and adapting to the situation in modern-day Guadeloupe. Those who cherish the language, instead of looking to the past, should be accepting this change and anticipating it by inventing and creating its modernity. You see, I am very careful what I say for my thoughts on Creole are far from complete. They are only just beginning. But I can relate to the Creole language like any writer living on the island.

AUTREMENT. Was Africa a mere stage in your life or does it still influence your writing and imagination?

MARYSE CONDÉ. I have been violently attacked and misunderstood, most unfairly, and suffered a great deal. I shall no longer try to justify myself. My response is simply that my criticism of Africa represented the full extent of my love for it and that we are always very strict with the ones we love. I believe that I loved Africa enormously and that I had every right to suffer from certain aspects of its politics and from certain cultural misadventures. And that's final. Today Africa is for me the presence of a past—in other words, I have understood the distance between me, an Antillean, and African culture. At the same time, however, it was Africa that revealed me to myself and allowed me, Maryse Condé, a Guadeloupean woman living in

Guadeloupe, to know who I am. Africa is inside me yet removed from me. I don't know how to explain this contradiction of belonging yet knowing too that I have left it for good and for excellent reasons. I shall no longer speak or write about it. Furthermore, as I have just said, creation is a kind of perpetual movement and I am not going to spend my time locked in *Segu*, behind its mud walls, narrating the past. Together with this self-awareness and the beauty and wealth of the Black World that Africa has given me and without which I would be nothing but a copy of the French, a copy of the white world, with no exact identity, I am going to continue to write and speak of the world from my point of view. Not just the Caribbean or Guadeloupean world but anything I can relate to. Anything which inspires me to write. It is Africa that has allowed me to see, with my own eyes, the world in which I live and to look at things round me in my own way, I Maryse Condé, black, female and Caribbean.

Living on My Island, Guadeloupe

As for Bert, he could stand it no longer. He wandered the night and space as far as the coastline, trying to glimpse in the distance that forbidden island sprawled in the middle of the ocean blue.

He wept:

'Dead or alive, will I always have arms too short to reach happiness?'

Maryse Condé, *Tree of Life*

These words by the hero of my last novel *Tree of Life* could very well have been my own because for thirty-three years Guadeloupe was always present in my dreams. As soon as I fell asleep I dreamt I was drifting in the ocean until I eventually reached an unknown island which turned out to be my native island of Guadeloupe. And in the very middle of the strange landscape of the mangrove I discovered the

Originally published as 'Habiter ce pays, la *Guadeloupe*', *Chemins Critiques* 1(3) (December 1989): 5–14, introduced by the following editorial note: 'This text by novelist Maryse Condé was written under extremely difficult conditions, when Hurricane Hugo wreaked devastation on Guadeloupe. The novelist, whose house was damaged, was unable to write the article she had first promised. Wanting, however, to keep her word, she forwarded this text on tape which we have transcribed with the hope that we have been able to translate the vivacity and spontaneity of her words.'

house where I was born and, oddly enough, the garden where I grew up with two flame trees on the edge of the street and an ylang-ylang tree to the left of the house.

For thirty-three years, therefore, living on my island for me was a fantasy, a dream that haunted me. When in 1986 I decided to return and settle on the island, I had to rediscover it and for me that was a totally new experience.

Living on this island is to live with a nature that I knew nothing about. I believe that every Caribbean child has never related to the nature round her. For her, the forest, the mangrove, the hibiscus and the bougainvillea were fixed elements of a décor which she took for granted.

Back in the Caribbean, after long years spent in the Sahel, a semi-desert region where the palette ranges from ochre to brown, where the trees are practically leafless—everyone knows the picture of the gnarled baobabs and those birds of the desert, the vultures, perched on their branches—I had to rediscover this nature and name every tree.

Living on this island meant, first of all, naming it. To know the ironwood, mastwood, silk cotton, mapou and locust trees. To name the trees of the forest one by one and re-appropriate them. Then to rediscover the mangrove and the coast of Guadeloupe, the beaches of grey volcanic and white sand, the madreporic cliffs, the brushwood and grasses. I was given a major lesson of things, as they used to tell me at school. And this re-appropriation of nature went hand in hand with a re-appropriation of the language because, of course, the trees have erudite Latin names but also, in most cases, Creole names.

I had to relearn as well these unfamiliar Creole names and the poetry that went with them. I listened, for example, to people talking to me of oilcloth flower, little star jasmine, goosefoot and morning glory. Talking about trees, they would speak of crabwood, cigar cedar and manjack. In other words, it was not simply nature that I was learning, re-learning, but also its words and its voice. There was a kind of correspondence (I'm not the one who invented the term) that emerged between the aspects of nature and the names it was given, which was absolutely captivating. I realized that all these trees I had grown up with but was unable to name had finally become an integral part of me. To re-appropriate nature, therefore, and its way of speaking was very important. Then, within this re-appropriation, nature had to be understood. Nature in the Caribbean has a personality all of its own. We have just endured a hurricane, for example, Hurricane Hugo which devastated the entire island. As a result, we might think that nature in the Caribbean is dangerous and hostile. I simply believe that it has a life of its own and its own rules about which we know nothing.

And this reminds me of a kind of African animism (the word is not quite right but must make do for want of something better), an animism I knew when I lived in the Sahel which teaches you to come to terms with nature. We have to learn to know nature, to name it but to also reconcile ourselves with it. In other words, re-establish between nature and man the links which religion, especially Catholicism, has broken. We have to learn how to tame the wind or else call upon it if need be. We have to learn how to make it rain or ask it to stop if there is too much. And all this pantheism, this animism which I knew nothing about while I was growing up in Guadeloupe, I felt like re-inventing it. I felt like re-inventing the mysterious links between everything round me and the temple of nature.

I also believe there are privileged elements of this nature, water for example, not only the waters of the rivers (I live next to the river Moustique) but also of the ocean. Obviously, we know the symbolism of water, the nurturing element, but perhaps in the Caribbean we have forgotten this aspect.

I see, for example, that the rivers like the one near my house are deserted and are only used in catastrophic events, like the one we have just experienced, when we have to go down to fill our buckets and draw water. But we no longer attach great importance to rivers. We let them flow and take them for granted. I think this pantheism which we have lost should be re-appropriated but without falling into a naive or puerile veneration. The word pantheism—which I use for want of a better word—is especially important as it implies a kind of mythology of the island and the Caribbean. Visitors to Guadeloupe often ask as they look at the Soufrière: 'In the past, did you ever consider this volcano a god? Are there any legends about it?' Obviously, we tend to find these questions somewhat paternalistic or folksy and as a rule we reply a bit curtly: 'No, we have never considered the Soufrière a god.' But perhaps our answer is a bit too hasty. There are links and relationships between our ancestors and nature that we don't know of and that perhaps we should look into. We have also completely obliterated the sacred aura of nature except for some minor elements. And if we compare what is happening in Guadeloupe to what is happening in a nearby island such as Haiti, where trees are considered the *loas'* resting place or associated with major religious ceremonies, we realize that we have considerably divested ourselves of the relationship we should be having with our environment. It is, of course, not a question of fabricating the past but we could conduct some sort of research and attempt to discover exactly what existed in the past. As a writer, I believe it would be of particular interest and serve as an enormous source of enrichment for literary creation.

I also believe that it would give power and a new complexity to our literature.

I said earlier that to recognize and re-appropriate the nature of the Caribbean means to also recognize and re-appropriate the Creole language.

I belong to that middle class which has been widely criticized and for whom Creole was a forbidden language. As a result of the life I led in Africa, where I met very few people from the Antilles, Creole had become somewhat secondary in my life, not to say non-existent.

Back home, I was forced to learn it again and wrap myself in another way of relating to people and things. I had to learn again how to speak with the inhabitants of Montebello about themselves, about myself and about the influence of nature that surrounded us. And I have to say that such an apprenticeship was by no means easy.

I shall not go into the quarrel between scholars and experts on the possible demise of Creole. Personally, I don't believe it. I simply believe that Creole is alive and well and now loaded with French words although that is not at all the sign of its demise or fossilized state. On the contrary, it is a sign of its very dynamic nature. There is, of course, that famous example quoted by Glissant about the fisherman who used to say 'mwen gen you zen' and who now no longer uses the same expression. I don't think it matters. I think what matters is that there is always a constantly renewed language which is resistant to French, which stands up to French as a valid adversary. So whether Creole becomes Frenchified or not is not important for me since it continues to be the preferred linguistic vehicle for most of the population.

So, I had to relearn Creole and you can imagine what that means for a writer. I must say straightaway, in order to avoid any demagogy, that I have never considered writing in Creole, although I increasingly plan to introduce into French all the sounds and metaphors and images imposed on me by the new environment and nature in which I live.

I would very much like the critics, when they read my next novel *Crossing the Mangrove* to tell me whether there has been any progress, for want of a better word, whether there has been any change in my writing compared to when I wrote *Segu* and when I was wrapped in African sonorities.

Living on this island means relearning to write, changing almost completely my way of writing.

Living on this island also means relearning a certain social fabric. I believe we all have a certain image of the Caribbean which borders on folklore, especially with regard to the relationship between old people and children, parents and children and men and women. We must come to realize, however, that the island is changing. For better or for worse, the Guadeloupe of 'long, long ago' no longer exists. Of course, the family structure in Guadeloupe remains somewhat unique for the woman is head of the family and she lives with several children by different fathers or by a single father who is generally absent. But it should be said that even this type of family is fast disappearing. The Antillean woman is changing; she has become less passive and more combative; she has learnt a certain number of things, including family planning. Since

I live in the country, I am talking about the girls I know. They practise birth control and know full well that they will not have eight or ten children like their mothers. It is also good to know that the boys who continue to be labelled macho with no respect or concern for women are also changing.

We must live on this island, therefore, and turn our gaze away from the past, away from the reassuring image that faithfully reflects a myth of the Caribbean which had us believe that we are different from the others and in possession of an easily identifiable identity. We must understand that the island is changing, that relations between individuals are changing and that a new Guadeloupe is emerging. Living on this island means to listen to modernity.

The other day I was rereading Fanon, whom we can never reread enough, and in Chapter 4 of his *Wretched of the Earth* he writes that the culture which the colonized intellectual is preoccupied with is nothing but a 'visible veneer', an inventory of particularisms. Culture goes much deeper and is the reflection of a dense, subterranean life in perpetual renewal, very difficult to define or simplify. At the very moment when we take into account Fanon's 'visible veneer', a people's true culture is already changing and being transformed. It is, therefore, very difficult to speak of culture since we are speaking of something in perpetual movement which contradicts you at the very moment when you want to turn it into a fixture.

Living on this island, therefore, means living something which is new, something which disconcerts you, something which calls out to you on every level. What makes Guadeloupe remain what it is despite everything, despite the fact that blood ties between Guadeloupe and the *métropole* are on the increase. For there is not a single Guadeloupean family which does not have relatives in France. Yet Guadeloupean identity is not deeply affected by it. Even with this constant contribution of foreign elements, its culture remains different from French culture, different from 'the Other'.

We have to study, therefore, the mechanism whereby we integrate so many things which appear the opposite of what we are, the mechanism by which we transform these things, absorb them and whereby we produce a culture which constantly represents a kind of challenge because we are so small, so pathetic. And that, in spite of all that, we remain absolutely different.

Living on this island, therefore, means solving the enigma of the remaining cultural particularisms.

I am not at all one of those people who believe that Guadeloupean culture is in the process of dying. I believe that it has never been so alive and well. But those who think it should be measured in terms of the past will be disappointed, since that past is dead and buried. Today, it is a question of speaking and writing in the present.

Living on this island, therefore, means speaking of it in the present, writing about it in the present. Which leads me to the question: What must we say in our books?

With some other writers I once attended a conference in Capesterre Belle-Eau where we were asked by a group of fifteen- and sixteen-year-olds: 'You always tell the same stories. We would like you to say something new. Why don't you write science fiction?' Obviously, we were unable to come up with an answer. We realized that the youth of Guadeloupe who live in the present, who live in the cultural present, want us to write about Guadeloupe as it is today—not about how we used to see it and not about how we would like it to be. It is terribly difficult to find a way of speaking about this island such as it is, to render its modernity and integrate it with the memories and remnants of this past which we cherish and would like to recreate. To be both in the present and guardian of a lost past, without which the present would lose its vitality and flavour, is a formidable task.

But, above all, living on this island means being constantly solicited politically. I believe that culture cannot be separated from politics. Living on this island means seeing for oneself the glaring, crying-out-loud inequalities. Since Hurricane Hugo, the screen of trees that masked so much misery has fallen. We can now see vast zones of shanty towns, the shacks patched with corrugated iron, wooden planks and shoddy wood. Poverty has turned up everywhere. And I think it's extraordinary to see the island naked, this island which for long boasted of the highest standard of living in the Caribbean, which looked down on its neighbours, the Haitians, the Dominicans and Jamaicans, and considered itself a kind of showcase for France and soon Europe. And to realize that we have been lied to by the politicians. The island is poor. Today we have twenty-five thousand victims of the disaster. But how many people lived in misery, on family allowances, before? We knew that the island lived on aid and that most people, in fact, lived solely on allowances, but we, the middle class, we never realized to what extent we were isolated from the terrible living conditions of the great majority of our fellow islanders. Everyone living on the island should be given what he deserves. This is not the discourse of a political campaign but simply the words of a Guadeloupean woman who was living in a highly privileged environment and now that, thanks to Hugo, the masks are off, has discovered her poverty-stricken fellow islanders.

Living on this island, therefore, means living a major injustice and enormous suffering for a great many people. Living on this island means endeavouring to establish more justice with equal access for all to better health, education and housing.

For a writer all this causes a kind of personal distress that has an impact on his work. Must this desire for justice and equality bring us back to the committed literature of the 1920s and 30s or post-Sartre? I believe we should have the courage to say that the committed literature, such as we once imagined it, should be banished. The writer is not a social theoretician. The writer is not a politician. The role of the writer is not to write ideological pamphlets in favour of such and such a party or denounce such- and-such a social or political system. I believe that the writer integrates a number of denunciations and demands in his writing, but this must never be his main aim or the primordial purpose of his work. A writer's aim is quite simply to try and recreate life. A writer's aim is to portray nothing more than the life round him in all its complexity and strangeness.

A few years ago, Georges Pérec wrote a wonderful book called *Life: A User's Manual* ([1978] 1987).[1] I believe that every one of our novels—I say novel because I am a novelist—is a response to the questions: How can we understand life, how can we talk about life and how can we live it?

1 Georges Pérec, *La Vie mode d'emploi* (Paris: Hachette, 1978). Available in English as *Life: A User's Manual* (David Bellos trans.) (Boston, MA: David R. Godine, 1987).

There is one absolutely indispensable element for the human mind and that is the faculty to dream. I believe that the writer must provide the dream to those who read her. Not a dream that is a refuge from reality or from the struggle we might undertake in life but simply a dream that is part of life. There is no life without dreams. There is no reality without dreams and by recreating life the writer also recreates dreams. For a certain time we considered this dimension of literature shameful. We privileged a certain type of writing. We despised a certain type of literary work and I now believe we should realize that this was unfortunate and that writing should be as complex as possible. It should integrate various aspects of reality and meet all the demands of the human heart.

So, finally, living on this island means re-thinking literature as well as the role of the writer. For a very long time we believed that the writer was a privileged individual, whereas in islands like ours a writer is not really recognized as an indispensable element of society. The inhabitants of Montebello, for example, don't understand what I do, sitting at home all day. Those who leave to go to work in the morning and come back in the afternoon don't understand that what I do is also called 'work'. I believe that living on this island leads us to a kind of modesty with regard to the function and status of the writer. A writer is merely someone who works in a different way from other people. Not in a nobler or more affected way but simply in a different way. On an island like ours, a writer is a man or woman like any other, listening to the island in a somewhat special way, endeavouring to express the voice of the island with his or her words, with his or her imagination and his or her sensitivity. The time when he or she was a privileged individual is long gone.

Living on this island, therefore, reminds us of this humility.

On the Other Side, Another *Country*
AFRICA AS SEEN BY AFRICAN AMERICAN WRITERS

In 1954, accepting an offer from his friend George Padmore, father of Pan-Africanism and political advisor to Kwame Nkrumah (then prime minister), Richard Wright set off for the Gold Coast. At the time, the Gold Coast appeared to offer the fascinating example of an emerging nation, an apprentice to democracy and industrialization, turning its back on a past steeped in feudalism and religiosity.

But the question remains whether Wright, American, writer and Marxist renegade, was sufficiently prepared to undertake such a trip. His political opinions prepared him no doubt to be interested in the career of a nationalist like Nkrumah. Apart from that, one of his biographers, Michel Fabre, tells us that, before undertaking such a trip, Wright read historian Eric Williams, English anthropologist Robert Sutherland Rattray, Eva Meyetovitz and Kofi Abrefa Busia, which seems to indicate the approach of a conscientious traveller gathering information about the country he is soon to visit. But it is evident that Wright never considered himself a traveller, much less a conscientious one, for he was black. And this journey by a black man to Africa of

Originally published as 'De l'autre bord, un autre pays', *Politique Africaine* 15 (*Images de la diaspora noire*) (September 1984): 34–47.

which he knew nothing thus instantly became the journey of a privileged witness researching the land of his origins.

Origins—the word is out!

What does *Black Power* ([1954] 2008), the fruit of his experience, tell us?[1] On its publication in America, it was greeted with a great many press reviews, most of them negative. Let us leave to one side all those who accused Wright of being unfair to British colonialism, of mercilessly denouncing its mercantile greed on which it was founded, of not even sparing the sacrosanct missionary work for his attacks. Let us leave to one side those who criticized him for dismissing Marxists and Capitalists by warning Nkrumah to be wary of everyone: 'Have no illusion regarding Western attitudes.'[2] Above all, let us recall David E. Apter writing in the *Chicago Sunday Tribune* on 10 October 1954: 'Wright was not seeking to find out about Gold Coast life and problems, but was searching for his own soul. [. . .] *Black Power* is by a person of great artistry and deep moral purpose. We cannot question his sincerity and emotion, but can only conclude that the people of Africa deserve more sober understanding.'

We couldn't have said it better. *Black Power* can be considered as revealing an autobiography as *Black Boy* (1944), a painful journey into the depths of his unconscious.[3] The book mercilessly reveals to us his horror of the religious ceremonies and rites of Africa, his unwitting contempt for

1 Richard Wright, *Black Power. Three Books from Exile: Black Power*; *The Color Curtain*; *and White Man, Listen!* (New York: HarperCollins, 2008).

2 Ibid., p. 411.

3 Richard Wright, *Black Boy: A Record of Childhood and Youth* (New York: HarperCollins, 2007).

its traditional institutions and his disgust at the dirt and misery which at the time was the lot of most people. Wasn't his analysis of the educated African, following a visit to Busia, the expression of his own tragic experience? 'The more he learns,' he wrote, 'the more Africa fades from his mind, and the more shameful and bizarre it seems.'[4]

As for the letter to Nkrumah which concludes his book, it is not simply pompous—'My journey's done. My labors in your vineyard are over'—it is perfectly arrogant.[5] Perhaps he was right to advocate the militarization of Africa, but when he writes 'I am an American and my country too was once a colony of England,' it is obvious that, in spite of himself, he has integrated a patriotic pride which his race could have protected him from.[6] Unintentionally and perhaps unknowingly, Wright was also the spiritual son of Ralph Waldo Emerson, the Puritan who championed the values of individualism and self-reliance. Let us be careful, however, not to blame the great writer. In his complexity, generosity, limitations and incoherence, Wright reflected the black American conscience in its relations with Africa.

AFRICA LOST AND FOUND

In *Blues People*: *Negro Music in White America* (1963), Amiri Baraka (formerly LeRoi Jones and Imamu Amiri Baraka) writes: 'The black middle class from its inception (possibly ten seconds after the first Africans were herded off the boat) has formed almost exclusively round the proposition that it is better not to be black in a country where being

4 Wright, *Black Power*, p. 284.

5 Ibid., p. 409.

6 Ibid., p. 420.

black is a liability.'[7] And he adds a little later: 'It was the growing black middle class who believed that the best way to survive in America would be to disappear *completely*, leaving no trace at all that there had ever been an Africa or a slavery or even finally a black man.'[8]

With his customary cruel irony, Baraka described the state of mind of every black American, if we accept that the proletariat and exploited of every category share the ideals and ideology of the middle class. For a long time the history of the black peoples in America was conceived in terms of progression and ascension. First, slavery, i.e. the night and the shame. Then emancipation, i.e. integration into the great American nation. When did things begin to change? Nathan Huggins reveals the ambiguity in reasserting the value of the African heritage, the basis of this movement in the 1920s.[9] We know that one of the high points of the short glorious history of Harlem was the march through the streets by the 369th infantry regiment composed solely of black Americans returned from war in Europe and awarded the Croix de Guerre. For a moment, the black peoples believed they could become heroes in America—provided they proved their strength or their creativity. And Alain Locke summoned the 'New Negro' to rehabilitate the race in the eyes of the world. And in order to determine a future whose lines remain to be defined, one must determine one's past.[10]

7 LeRoi Jones (Imamu Amiri Baraka), *Blues People: Negro Music in White America* (New York: William Morrow and Sons, 1963), p. 123–4.

8 Ibid.

9 See Nathan Irvin Huggins, *Harlem Renaissance,* updated edn (New York: Oxford University Press, 2007).

10 See Alain LeRoy Locke (ed.), *The New Negro: Voices of the Harlem Renaissance* (New York: Simon and Schuster, 1992).

In a movement somewhat similar to the one occurring today in Guadeloupe and Martinique, some turned to the oral heritage. We shall not recall here the wealth of black America's oral traditions which, except for the field of music, some are calling dead and buried. As early as the end of the nineteenth century, Joel Chandler Harris published his Uncle Remus stories—*Uncle Remus: His Songs and His Sayings* (1880) and *Nights with Uncle Remus* (1881)—to name a few, whose central character was Bre'er Rabbit who is not, far from it, the only hero of the tales.[11] Must we, however, limit ourselves to compiling stories and songs, even with love and respect, whose nature is constantly threatened by a changing society? Shouldn't we, on the contrary, make use of them to nurture personal creation? The question is important and Arthur Fauset blamed Zora Neale Hurston, like Joel Chandler Harris before her, for taking dangerous liberties with oral material. A controversial character of the Harlem Renaissance, forgotten and then rediscovered by Alice Walker in the 1970s, Zora Neale Hurston is at the centre of this debate. She had a very exact idea of literature's role, especially black literature. Its role was to illustrate the inherent dynamism of the Black World despite the race problem. 'We talk about the race problem a great deal,' she wrote, 'but go on living and laughing and striving like everybody else.'[12] She tended to somewhat minimize the tensions and conflicts of country life in the

11 See Joel Chandler Harris, *The Complete Tales of Uncle Remus* (New York: Houghton Mifflin, 2002 [1955]). Parts of the collection are also available at amazon.com as free downloads for Kindle.

12 'Zora Neale Hurston on Zora Neale Hurston' in Cheryl A. Wall (ed.), *Their Eyes Were Watching God: A Casebook* (New York: Oxford University Press, 2000), p. 18.

South in her folktales from Florida, *Mules and Men* (1935).[13] Voices as authoritative as the poet Sterling Brown criticized her for it, stating that any work written by a black person should, on the contrary, recreate, even accentuate, the bitterness of the black peoples' condition in America. Likewise, her novel *Their Eyes Were Watching God* (1937), which Alice Walker claimed as the most important book in her eyes, was criticized by intellectual luminaries of the time, especially Locke, for not being faithful to reality.[14]

What reality?

The objective reality of the black peoples' living conditions? A reality totally subjective and interior? Reality for whom? Reality for what? All these questions and many others were soon to be echoed a thousand times.

WHAT IS THE PROMISED LAND?

The Harlem Renaissance generated the birth of a remarkable group of writers, most of them poets. Today, more than Langston Hughes and his poems written to a jazz rhythm, the prize goes to Jean Toomer, the author of *Cane* (1923).[15] His is a complex work, both polemic and poetic, bold in form and often disconcerting since there is no obvious unity of writing or theme. Composed of a series of sketches, vignettes and stories, it creates an overall picture both psychological and physical only once the book is closed. But, even in the author's opinion, *Cane* was a swansong and that

13 See Zora Neale Hurston, *Mules and Men* (New York: Harper and Row, 1990).

14 See Zora Neale Hurston, *Their Eyes Were Watching God* (New York: HarperCollins, 2000).

15 See Jean Toomer, *Cane*, new edn (New York: Liveright, 2011).

makes it doubly symbolic since Toomer repudiated his belonging to the Black World. This transformation antici-pated in an extreme form what the majority of black American writers were soon to realize—that the rehabili-tation of their African heritage would not be enough to nourish their literary work. Hence, they began to scour the infinity of their own selves. Without ever turning their backs on the race problem and the harsh reality of black–white relations, black American writers discovered that Africa was no longer a reference of origin, functioning as a myth. Paradoxically, however, though Africa and the African heritage ceased to be clearly claimed objects of desire, they never stopped invading the literary field, so to speak. In his preface to *Manchild in the Promised Land* (1965), Claude Brown thus writes:

> I want to talk about the first Northern urban gen-eration of Negroes. I want to talk about the expe-riences of a misplaced generation, of a misplaced people in an extremely complex, confused society. This is a story of their searching, their dreams, their sorrows, their small and futile rebellions and their endless battle to establish their own place in America's greatest metropolis—and in America itself.[16]

And we can think of the history of this generation and the culture born out of it as an avatar of the rural culture of the South, itself an avatar of slavery, itself an avatar of the culture of Africa. This searching, these dreams, these sorrows, these battles and rebellions are very much those of an Africa which refuses or attempts (it boils down to the

16 See Claude Brown, *Manchild in the Promised Land* (New York: Scribner, 2012), p. ix.

same) to lose itself, as Baraka writes in *Blues People*, in a vague America with no definite contours.

Although Richard Wright was considered to be the major novelist of the 1940s in America, 'the first black to write a bestseller', he was eclipsed by James Baldwin and Ralph Ellison. Let us consider for a moment Baldwin who violently criticized Wright's aesthetic and conception of literature before in turn being violently taken to task by Eldridge Cleaver in *Soul on Ice* (1968), proving that he too perfectly symbolized a moment in the conscience of 'this misplaced people' mentioned by Claude Brown—the conviction that the African legacy had vanished and that it was the white man's which had to be blindly appropriated despite its deformation of a certain Africanity.[17]

Baldwin's work is usually seen as an exaltation of individuality, of an individual experience which nourishes the general fate of a people. Baldwin, however, seemed to underscore the impossibility of fulfilling this individuality on either a racial or sexual level. More than any other, even in times when his activism seemed particularly virulent, he never stopped believing in a force of redemption which would sweep even through the white community—love. It is love that would bring together blacks and whites, homosexuals and heterosexuals, so as to put an end to the 'racial nightmare' that America was living. This theory is especially evident in *Another Country* (1960) where the complex and morbid love patterns of Rufus, Leona, Ida and Eric are supposed to portray a society which will be born out of the bitterness of the present.[18] Love, however, is first

17 See Eldridge Cleaver, *Soul on Ice* (New York: Random House, 1999).

18 See James Baldwin, *Another Country* (New York: Vintage, 1993).

of all the reconciliation with oneself in a somewhat painful discovery of one's identity. And *Go Tell It on the Mountain* (1952) is in fact a search, not so much for God but for one-self, accepting one's darker sides as well as the few glimpses of light.[19] The characters of the 'righteous', the father and his first wife, Deborah, are nothing but shams, guilty of not being able to accept themselves, sinners that only love can save. The 'sinners', however, are out of the shadows and into the light and certain one day to be 'saints'. And what about Africa? It is precisely the splinter that keeps the wound open. This misplaced people who are seeking to dialogue with God, with the Other, and assert their creativity are, in fact, interacting with their origins, with the Africa within themselves and working to transmute it into a force of which they can be proud. Critics have highlighted Baldwin's language as a creation as 'black' as jazz. Interviewed on the topic, the writer has admitted a number of influences: 'The King James Bible, the rhetoric of the store-front church, something ironic and violent and perpetually understated in Negro speech.'[20] Baldwin's writing is said to be in the direct tradition of tales from the South as well as the songs and preaching of true pastors or impostors.

Africa itself, however, was changing. Added to the traditional and tragic images of the slave trade and the tortured slave were those of its martyrs such as Patrice Lumumba, its leaders such as Kwame Nkrumah and intellectuals of all kinds. They infused a new dynamic into

19 See James Baldwin, *Go Tell It on the Mountain* (New York: Dell, 2000).

20 James Baldwin, 'Autobiographical Notes' in *Notes of a Native Son* (New York: Dial Press, 1984[1955]), pp. 7–12; here, p. 9.

African thought, shattering, for example, the theological and political discourse. In *The Fire Next Time* (1963), Baldwin writes of his meeting with the black Muslims of Elijah Muhammad and one quote comes to mind, which he addresses in thought to Elijah: 'I love a few people and they love me, and some of them are white, and isn't love more important than color?'[21]

We know that this gospel of love was to be belied by facts. Martin Luther King and Malcolm X proved it with their assassinations. But, before he died, Malcolm X founded the Organization of Afro-American Unity destined to symbolize the luminous reintegration of Africa into black America. And this reintegration, this superimposition of old and new images, not only shattered the theological and political discourse but also modified the literary field. This was the time for autobiographies, testimonies and resounding conversions, all following the same pattern—from a painful, shameful Africanity, engendering hatred of self and all kinds of searching, to the assumption of Africa within ourselves, i.e. self-reconciliation, such as is evident in the autobiographies of Malcolm X, Eldridge Cleaver and the Soledad Brothers, as if fiction were better served by reality. Henceforth, the way was wide open for parody which, although it was not absent from black American writing (see certain pages of Ralph Ellison's *Invisible Man* [1952]),[22] was to culminate with Ishmael Reed and a few others.

21 James Baldwin, *The Fire Next Time* (New York: Vintage, 1993), p. 71.

22 Ralph Ellison, *Invisible Man* (New York: Vintage, 1995).

SWEET ARPEGGIO OF TEARS (MARI EVANS)

We will certainly be criticized for placing special emphasis on women's literature. But we are merely following a general trend. In her foreword to Robert E. Hemenway's biography of Zora Neale Hurston, Alice Walker writes that, up to a certain time, women were 'names appended, like verbal footnotes, to the illustrious all-male list that paralleled them.'[23] One of the finest books of black American literature, *Brown Girl, Brownstones* by Paule Marshall (1959), never obtained the recognition of Baldwin's *Go Tell It on the Mountain* published around the same time.[24] As we said, it required the passionate efforts of Walker to bring back the writings of Hurston who had been totally forgotten among the Harlem Renaissance writers. One of the most spectacular events of recent years, however, has been the emergence, we could even say the supremacy, of women in black American literature. The place and role of women in black America has always been the subject of controversy and the image of the black American female has been overshadowed by contradiction and incoherence. Sometimes she is pictured as a sexual object, sometimes as the driving resistance to cultural alienation. People like Angela Davis even see in her domestic chores a demonstration of her essential gifts and her liberating strength:

> Precisely through performing the drudgery which
> has long been a central expression of the socially
> conditioned inferiority of women, the Black

23 Alice Walker, 'Zora Neale Hurston: A Cautionary Tale and a Partisan View'. Foreword to Robert E. Hemenway, *Zora Neale Hurston: A Literary Biography* (Champaign: University of Illinois Press, 1980), pp. xi–xviii; here, p. xii.

24 Paule Marshall, *Brown Girl, Brownstones* (New York: Dover, 2009).

woman in chains could help to lay the foundation for some degree of autonomy, both for herself and her men. Even as she was suffering under her unique oppression as female, she was thrust into the center of the slave community. She was, therefore, essential to the *survival* of the community.[25]

As a rule, whereas black American male writers strive to illustrate the confrontation of the black and white worlds and denounce racism and its effects on the black psyche, women writers take special interest in the closed world of the black community, out of reach of the white world. There is perhaps a signifcant reason for this. Black women are sensitive to the false image (deserving mother or whore, there is no alternative) given to them by both black and white men and reject it. All you need do is re-read *Go Tell It on the Mountain* to draw up a genuine inventory of masculine representations of women.

Women writers (Alice Walker, Paule Marshall, Toni Cade Bambara, Toni Morrison, Rosa Guy, Louise Merriwether or Gloria Naylor) give a very different image of the black American female and this is what we shall deal with here because the role they mean to play by choosing their words, the relation they intend to form with their readers, in short, their concept of literature, is a way of broaching the Africa within themselves.

Critic Addison Gayle took Toni Morrison's second novel *Sula* (1974)[26] to task, claiming that Morrison was taking

25 Angela Davis, 'Reflection on the Black Woman's Role in the Community of Slaves', *The Black Scholar* 3(4) (November–December 1981): 2–16; here, p. 7. Also available in Joy James (ed.), *The Angela Y. Davis Reader* (Malden, MA: Blackwell, 1999), pp. 111–28.

26 See Toni Morrison, *Sula* (New York: Alfred A. Knopf, 2002).

responsibility for the stereotypes belonging to a certain Negritude strangely similar to the Harlem Renaissance: 'Black art must create images, symbols and metaphors of positive import from the Black experience [. . .] and must divorce itself from the sociological attempt to explain the Black community in terms of pathology.'[27]

The criticism does not seem justified to us. The goal that Morrison sets herself is clear—it consists of building a myth, i.e. integrating the positive and negative aspects of black culture and creating an allegory of black history in America which recreates all the ambiguities. Like any other community, the black American community has pathological aspects inherent to its functioning. Gayle therefore refers to a didactic vision of literature which Morrison has nothing to do with. Morrison takes the deliberate risk of highlighting the negative aspects of black culture instead of covering them up and valorizing the finished product. Isn't this the obvious sign of her creative freedom which is now capable of assessing and interpreting her cultural heritage? Those who are bent on tracking Africa in Morrison's work, like following a trail strewn with white stones, risk being disappointed. In *Song of Solomon* (1977), for example, it is the meaning of Milkman's search for his family's place of origin, the place where his firstborn flew to the lost continent:

> Solomon done fly, Solomon done gone,
> Solomon cut across the sky, Solomon gone home.[28]

27 Addison Gayle, 'Blueprint for Black Criticism', *Black World* 1(1) (1977): 41–5; here, p. 43. Also available in Nathaniel Norment Jr (ed.), *The Addison Gayle Jr Reader* (Champaign: University of Illinois Press, 2009), pp. 159–69.

28 Toni Morrison, *Song of Solomon* (New York: Vintage, 2004), p. 303.

But to treat the African presence in this book as a mere referent would be to seriously mutilate it. Africa is hidden away somewhere in the language, the heroes' psychology and gestures and what does it matter if this hiding place is inaccessible? It mirrors the African presence in this black soul remodelled by three centuries of transplantation.

Those who seek clear-cut images will get more satisfaction out of Alice Walker. In her short-story collections, *In Love and Trouble* (1977) and *You Can't Keep a Good Woman Down* (1982), the African referent is omnipresent.[29] In the first, for example, we leaf through the diary of an African nun:

> Our mission school is at the foot of lovely Uganda mountains and is a resting place for travelers. Classrooms in daylight, a hotel when the sun sets.
>
> The question is in the eyes of all who come here: Why are you—so young, so beautiful (perhaps)— a nun?[30]

And this nun will discover that the type of life she has adopted, the religion she has made her own, forbids her the wonderful gift of motherhood, the symbol of creativity. In other words, she will discover that the West gags and muzzles the Black World.

Leafing through the pages we find certain descriptions: 'The women in Jerome's group wore short kinky

---

29 See Alice Walker, *In Love and Trouble: Stories of Black Women* (New York: Harvest, 2004) and *You Can't Keep a Good Woman Down* (New York: Harvest, 2004).

30 Alice Walker, 'The Diary of an African Nun' in *In Love and Trouble*, pp. 113–18; here, p. 113.

hair and large hoop earrings. They stuck together, calling themselves by their "African" names, and never went to church.'[31]

It is in *The Color Purple* (1982), however, that Walker combines most efficiently the double presence of Africa: Africa as referent and Africa transformed through transplantation.[32] In the exchange of letters between the two sisters, Nettie and Celie, it is not the dialogue that counts but the justification for Africa. Nettie has undertaken the return to Africa while Celie undergoes the life of exile and slavery that is the lot of the black American. In some places, the novel sounds more like an anthropological treatise: 'It was my first Olinka funeral. The women paint their faces white and wear white shroud-like garments and cry in a high keening voice. They wrapped the body in barkcloth and buried it under a big tree in the forest. Tashi was heartbroken.'[33]

Clichés and stereotypes are not lacking: 'The Africans' teeth remind me of horses' teeth, they are so fully formed, straight and strong.'[34]

Moreover, Celie, the sister who has remained in America, is the victim of misfortunes such as rape, beatings and all types of setbacks that would befit the heroine of an edifying anti-slavery novel. This collection of women, victims and whores, both resistant and passive, contributes nothing new to the panoply of black American heroines. But perhaps the novel's strength lies in appropriating almost

31 Alice Walker, 'Her Sweet Jerome' in *In Love and Trouble*, pp. 24–34; here, p. 31.

32 Alice Walker, *The Color Purple* (New York: Harvest, 2003).

33 Ibid., pp. 140–1.

34 Ibid., p. 149.

hackneyed material to make it into an innovating work, for *The Color Purple* is also a reflection on the relationship between Mother Africa and the diaspora: 'The Africans don't even see us, they don't even recognize us [. . .] We love them. We try every way we can to show that love. But they reject us. They never even listen to how we've suffered. And if they listen they say stupid things. Why don't you speak our language? They ask.'[35]

An affirmation of the distance that has grown between Africa and its diaspora. And a pathetic attempt to bridge the gap. Perhaps that is how we should interpret Tashi's return to America and the ellipsis of the last pages:

> What your people love best to eat over there in Africa? Us ast.
> She sort of blush and say barbecue.[36]

THE MOTHER TONGUE

If we admit, as Jacques Stephen Alexis puts it so well, that Africa never leaves the black man in peace, whatever his nationality, wherever he goes or comes from,[37] even if this harassment is often nothing more than a game of hide and seek, there is a place where its presence is inscribed loud and clear—language.

In their search for identity, black American writers have never minimized the linguistic dimension of acculturation. They therefore began to rehabilitate the speech of the slave, his songs and mimicry. Even W. E. B. Du Bois endeavoured to analyse this cultural aspect by highlighting

35 Ibid., p. 243.

36 Ibid., p. 244.

37 See Alexis, *General Sun, My Brother.*

the therapeutic value of words. He aptly pointed out that
words and their usage constituted techniques of survival.
The poets of the Harlem Renaissance went further. Using
the American vocabulary, they attempted to recreate the
very rhythm of black orality. Here is the poem by Langston
Hughes called 'Trumpet Player: 52nd Street' (1947):

> The Negro
> With the trumpet at his lips
> Has dark moons of weariness
> Beneath his eyes
> Where the smoldering memory
> Of slave ships
> Blazed to the crack of whips
> About his thighs.[38]

In other words, this generation endeavoured to rehabilitate, then restore, a specific type of communication
inherited from the time of slavery.

'Black music endured and grew as a communicative
language, as a sustaining spiritual force [. . .] and as a
creative extension of our African selves. It was one of the
few mediums of expression open to black people that
was virtually free of interference.'[39] Thus spoke Don L.
Lee, who changed his name to Haki Madhubuti, urging
poets of the 1960s never to lose sight of these effects and
to evoke them in their own writing. It was believed to be a

38 Langston Hughes, 'Trumpet Player: 52nd Street', *Mainstream*
(Winter 1949): 44–5. Also available as 'Trumpet Player' in Arnold
Rampersad (ed.), *The Collected Poems of Langston Hughes* (New York:
Vintage, 1995), pp. 338–9; here, p. 338.

39 Don L. Lee, 'Dynamite Voices I: Black Poets of the 1960s' in *Black
Books Bulletin* 1(4) (1973): 41.

done deal when, in 1981, Toni Cade Bambara, author of *The Salt Eaters* (1980), declared: 'There are a lot of aspects of consciousness for which there is no vocabulary, no structure in the English language which would allow people to validate that experience through language. [. . .] I'm trying to break words open and get at the bones.'[40]

The argument is subtly different. It is no longer a question of acting like an anthropologist in love with his research topic but to create and assemble signs faithful to vocalism and the meaning of black speech. Language is a living element that is constantly integrating a whole set of factors in the course of its history. It is this mobility that has to be captured and imprisoned between the ungrateful pages of a book. It is here that the poet Ntozake Shange meets up with Toni Cade Bambara in an attempt to break moulds, reinvent and rewrite. Here is an extract from *Sassafrass, Cypress & Indigo* (1982):

> i am sassafras / my fingers behold you
> i call upon you with my song you teach
> me in my sleep / i am not a besieger of yr
> fortress / i am a crusader / for you are
> all my past / i offer my body to
> make manifest yr will in this dungeon[41]

---

40 Toni Cade Bambara, *The Salt Eaters* (New York: Vintage, 1992). The quotation is from Kalamu Ya Salaam, 'Searching for the Mother Tongue: An Interview with Toni Cade Bambara', *First World* 2(4) (1980): 47–52; here, p. 48. The interview is also available in Thabiti Lewis (ed.), *Conversations with Toni Cade Bambara* (Jackson: University Press of Mississippi, 2012).

41 Ntozake Shange, *Sassafrass, Cypress & Indigo* (New York: Picador, 1996), p. 109.

It is obvious that this claim for a mother tongue different from English speech, 'stripped of the kinds of structures and the kinds of vocabularies that allow people to plug into other kinds of intelligences',[42] comprises a good deal of ambiguity for it is a solitary intellectual exercise, divorced by its very nature from the deep ties with the community that in theory inspires it. But doesn't this ambiguity match the distance which separates Africa from her children in America?

THE CREATION OF THE NEW WORLD

By way of a conclusion I would like to express a very personal opinion. To search for the image or presence of Africa in black American literature does not seem to be of great urgency. Of course, you can always call to the rescue such and such an African writer and draw parallels between his work and that of the black Americans. We can talk of similar rhythms and metaphors together with communication codes. We can even highlight the fact that, since African writers have interiorized, more than they'd like to admit, the cultural and linguistic models of the Western world, they are closer to their brothers in America and have to solve similar problems. But once this has been said, what new light have we cast?

To hunt for Africa in the literary work of black Americans boils down, to a certain degree, to questioning their creative capacity to defy diktats while speaking about themselves and the world. If the black American speaks of Africa, he is claiming an individual interest whose contours are defined by his sensitivity. If he doesn't speak of Africa

42 Toni Cade Bambara, in Salaam, 'Searching for the Mother Tongue'.

in clear terms, it is nevertheless present somewhere deep in his blood and inner self. It is one thing if Africa and its reality play a political role for black Americans who take ideological sides and want to contribute to the liberation and development of the continent. But literary creation is not a political discourse (even if it contains fragments) and black American literature gains little from being analysed with the tools of the sociologist and political scientist. It is much more rewarding in the end to address these works we have too briefly broached as the dynamic and precious expression of a certain Américanité.

The immense majority of black Americans, like the people from the Caribbean, no longer consider themselves *Africans in exile*, i.e. craving for Africa. On the contrary, they believe their origin adds to the wealth of their creativity in the land where they have put down roots.

Globalization and Diaspora

'O Brave New World'
Shakespeare, *The Tempest*

The word globalization seems sometimes synonymous with Americanism or Americanization, as James W. Ceaser remarks in *Reconstructing America* (1997), and raises negative images.[1] Globalization is said to be the death knell of authentic cultures and does away with national specificities as part of a shapeless magma. On the subject of Americanism, Martin Heidegger states that it is 'the still unfolding and not yet full or completed metaphysical essence of the emerging monstrousness of modern times'—it is homogenizing, erases specificities and is one-dimensional.[2] Extremists such as Alexandre Kojève go even further. It would mean the end of history. The countries of the Third World, especially from the Caribbean, would be perfect victims of this world order, lacking economic and political clout and making headlines only in the event of

Originally published as 'Globalization and Diaspora' (Jill Cairns trans.), *Diogène* 46(4) (October–December 1998): 29–36.

1 See James W. Ceaser, *Reconstructing America: The Symbol of America in Modern Thought* (New Haven, CT: Yale University Press, 1998).

2 Martin Heidegger, *Holzwege* (Frankfurt: Vittorio Klostermann, 1957), p. 103. Cited in Ceaser, *Reconstructing America*, p. 196.

natural disasters such as Hurricanes Hugo, George and Mitch. The little island of Montserrat, previously unknown to the West, got international attention only when its volcano, Soufrière Hills, decided to erupt. Rwanda became famous after the genocide and the Congo for its civil war and the assassination of its leader.

I do not fully share this unanimous pessimism. A certain form of globalization does not scare me. In the best of cases, the notion implies an expansion of linguistic and natural borders among the black communities of the world. As early as the Second World War, Paris witnessed the beginnings of a certain globalization. For many reasons, Paris had become the ideal terrain for the exchange and communication of ideas. This paradox deserves a closer look.

Paris was the capital of an immense empire, a place where colonial civil servants carved up Africa and subjugated millions of Africans. This did not prevent the Dahomeyan Kojo Touvalou-Quenum from describing it as the Promised Land for the children of Ham. In a speech called 'Paris, Heart of the Black Race', given in Liberty Hall in New York City, he wished for the French capital to become the Babel of the Black World.[3] French colonialism and primitivism combined oddly enough to promote a vision of black unity. We all know that it was in Paris that literary personalities as diverse as Langston Hughes, Countee Cullen, Jean Toomer, Claude Mckay, Jean Price-Mars, the young Aimé Césaire, Léopold Sédar Senghor and René Maran met. We also know that the Trinidadian, George Padmore, future father of Pan-Africanism, spent many

3 Kojo Touvalou-Quenum, 'Paris, coeur de la race noir', *Les Continents* 9 (September 1924).

long years in Paris where he met the French Soudanese Tiemoko Garan Kouyaté, editor of *La Race nègre*. Thanks to René Maran, Alain Locke discovered the young genera-tion of Francophone students. In December 1927, Jane Nardal, still a student, wrote to Locke, then professor at Howard University, asking for permission to translate *The New Negro* (1925), the collection of essays he had edited.[4] She offered the project to Payot, the well-known French editor, and suggested that her sister Paulette, a student of English, be in charge of the translation. Locke accepted and even offered to write a new introduction to the French version. Unfortunately, the project never materialized. Despite this setback, Nardal was to become the most important cultural intermediary between the Harlem Ren-aissance writers and the Francophone students who made up the core of the Negritude movement. With her friend, Léo Sajou, she founded the *Revue du monde noir* (1931–32) which became the focus of black cultural activity in Paris. We can regret that Jane and Paulette Nardal, who played an essential role in the initial efforts at globalizing black culture, have been so marginalized. Brent Hayes Edwards, a young American researcher, reminds us that Paulette Nardal complained bitterly of this marginalization in a let-ter to Jacques Hymans, written in 1963: 'Senghor and Césaire took up the ideas tossed out by us and expressed them with more flash and brio [. . .] We were but women, real pioneers—let's say that we blazed the trail for them.'[5]

4 Alain Locke (ed.), *The New Negro: Voices of the Harlem Renaissance* (Arnold Rampersad introd.) (New York: Touchstone, 1997).

5 Brent Hayes Edwards, *The Practice of Diaspora: Literature, Transla-tion, and the Rise of Black Internationalism* (Cambridge, MA: Harvard University Press, 2003), p. 122.

It was the same marginalization that Suzanne Césaire suffered a few years later. Despite her brilliant collaboration in the journal *Tropiques* (1940–44), the critics had no hesitation declaring that she was merely copying the ideas of her husband.

I consider these various elements—the friendship between Maran and Locke; the relationship between Padmore and Kouyaté; Jane Nardal's letter to Locke and his numerous articles in *La Dépêche Africaine* (1928–32)—as the first milestones of a positive globalization. At that time, black peoples had no intention of solving their problems individually. On the contrary, like Nardal, they advocated the transnationalization of black culture as the only solution:

> In this postwar period, the barriers that exist between countries are being lowered, or are being pulled down. Will the diversity of frontiers, tariffs, prejudices, customs, religions, and languages ever allow the realization of this project? We would like to hope so [. . .] Negroes of all origins and nationalities, with different customs and religions, vaguely sense that they belong, in spite of everything, to a single and same race.[6]

What was Negritude, what was Pan-Africanism, if not a form of globalization, a notion of total identity and active solidarity among black peoples? At the time, all the voices were unanimous. Only Fanon sowed a doubt: 'The only common denominator between the blacks from Chicago and the Nigerians or Tanganyikans was that they all defined themselves in relation to the whites.'[7]

6 Jane Nardal, 'L'internationalisme noir', *La Dépêche Africaine* 1 (February 1928): 5. Cited in ibid., p. 18.

7 Fanon, *The Wretched of the Earth*, pp. 153–4.

But no one paid attention to Fanon's warning and Race was declared sacrosanct. Fanon, however, was right. This notion of Race, which is so blinding, is in fact a legacy of the pseudo-scientific theories of the eighteenth and nineteenth centuries. Comte de Buffon, Guillaume Thomas Raynal and, later, the illustrious Comte de Gobineau had divided humanity into sub-groups, using colour as the essential criterion for their classification. For colonial reasons, the Indian and the African were placed on the last rung of the human ladder. There was even a debate as to whether the black man belonged to the species of apes or humans. This did not prevent black intellectuals in their exile or travels from being open to the host country: What would Claude McKay's *Banjo* (1929) be without its references to Marseilles? What would Nella Larsen's *Quicksand* (1928) be without its references to Copenhagen?[8] Likewise, Marxism, which so many black intellectuals embraced so devoutly and dreamt of, was nothing but the globalization of a world without borders whose foundations would no longer be Race but Class. Oppressed of the world, unite!

During the first quarter of the twentieth century, therefore, the intellectuals from the Caribbean, Africa and America were obsessed with dreams of transnationalization and globalization. It was the political developments of the African countries which were to put an end to these hopes. Most of the African countries gained independence around 1960. Many of the intellectuals who were the driving force of cultural life in Paris, like Senghor, went back home to occupy key positions. Each country withdrew

8 Claude McKay, *Banjo* (New York: Harvest, 1970); Nella Larsen, *Quicksand* (Santa Barbara: Praeger, 1970).

behind its borders and was concerned with its own development and safeguarding its own culture. The only exception was Nkrumah who remembered the Africanism of Garvey and gave his country the yellow, black and green flag. What is more, he invited W. E. B. Du Bois to come and live in Ghana as his second homeland. The situation in the Caribbean was more complex. Cuba seemed to achieve a victory over imperialism. The English-speaking islands gained independence. They endeavoured to pursue the dream of unity, but the Federation collapsed in 1962. As for the French-speaking islands, they became overseas departments in 1946 resulting in an increasing political, cultural and economic dependence on France. For all these reasons, the dream of Pan-Africanism died a natural death. The Africans fought for the rehabilitation of their own traditions, languages and religions. Perhaps necessary, they nevertheless constituted so many barriers to transnationalization. As a result, the notion of Race in some sectors was being replaced by that of Culture. Today, the Créolité movement in Martinique is a good illustration of keeping Africa on the sidelines in a culture of the diaspora and highlighting the plantation as matrix.

Globalization of the third millennium is perhaps a way of reviving the faded dream of unity. The migration factor is a prefiguration. Demographers tell us that migration is the dominant factor at the end of the twentieth century. The causes of this worldwide phenomenon are multiple. Some flee dictatorship and genocide. Others, poverty and despair. And yet others, religious fanaticism. Caribbean and African peoples no longer immigrate to their metropolises of colonization but settle in any country where they can hope to survive. We will not go into semantics here but should we call these immigrant communities 'diasporas'?

We agree with Stuart Hall when he states that the notion of diaspora implies new hybrid and syncretic identities as well as new multicultural spaces: '[D]iaspora does not refer us to those scattered tribes whose identity can only be secured in relation to some sacred homeland to which they must at all costs return, even if it means pushing other peoples into the sea. [. . .] Diaspora identities are those which are constantly producing and reproducing themselves anew, through transformation and difference.'[9]

Migration results in an increasing number of families composed on foreign soil and the phenomenon of the Second Generation born outside their parents' country of origin and incapable of identifying with it. It is unfair to treat these immigrant communities as dysfunctional (as is too often the case), living in a no-man's-land, rootless and with a confused sense of identity. As Marie-Céline Lafontaine writes, these communities are superficially imprisoned in a binary opposition: 'They seem to be either imitators or guardians of a heritage.'[10]

I claim that, on the contrary, these immigrant communities are a place of enrichment and the seat of an extraordinary creativity. Caribbean music has been revitalized in New York, Paris and London; and not only music. In *Borderlands*, Gloria Anzaldúa writes:

9 Stuart Hall, 'Cultural Identity and Diaspora' in J. Rutherford (ed.), *Identity: Community, Culture, Difference* (London: Lawrence and Wishart, 1990), pp. 222–37; here, p. 235.

10 Marie-Céline Lafontaine, 'Le Carnaval de l' "autre": A propos d' "authenticite" en matiere de musique guadeloupéenne, theories et réalités', *Les Temps Modernes* 441–2 (April–May 1983): 2126–73; here, p. 2144.

'The Aztecas del Norte compose the largest single tribe or nation of Anishinabeg (Indians) found in the United States today . . . Some call themselves Chicanos and see themselves as people whose true homeland is Aztlán [the US Southwest].'

[. . .]

The US-Mexican border *es una herida abierta* [is a place] where the Third World grates against the First and bleeds. And before a scab forms it hemorrhages again, the lifeblood of two worlds merging to form a third country—a border culture.[11]

A recent survey in the *New York Times* revealed that a growing number of men and women refuse the strict American classification of black/white and see themselves as belonging to a mixed race.[12] This means that *métissage*, miscegenation, which in the time of slavery and under colonial rule was considered the worst form of evil and a disorder in society's and nature's order of things, is now rehabilitated. The mixed blood is no longer seen as an inferior being but as the melting pot of multiple cultural values. Mexican poet and philosopher José Vasconcelos strongly opposes white America's doctrine of racial purity and sees a *raza mestiza*, a cosmic race, a fifth race embracing all the so-called races of the world.[13]

11 Jack D. Forbes, *Aztecas del Norte: The Chicanos of Aztlán* (Greenwich, CT: Premier Books, 1973), p. 30, cited in Anzaldúa, *Borderlands/La Frontera*, p. 1; Anzaldúa, *Borderlands/La Frontera*, p. 3.

12 Michael Lind, 'The Beige and the Black', *The New York Times*, 16 August 1998.

13 José Vasconcelos, *La raza cósmica. Misión de la raza iberoamericana. Notas de viajes a la América del Sur* (Madrid: Agencia mundial de librería, 1925).

Although much disparaged at the time, we should give Senghor his due since he reminded us that *métissage* is not merely biological and that, through colonization, we have become cultural hybrids.[14] Furthermore, today's scholars, taking the opposite view of the dubious systems elaborated in the eighteenth and nineteenth centuries, tell us they do not know what Race means. In 1950, a group of the world's leading researchers concluded in a UNESCO study that biological studies support the ethics of a universal brotherhood. It is perhaps time to renounce an obsolete vocabulary and seek to establish new definitions of the world's communities.

The individuals belonging to the Second Generation, the cultural hybrids, burst onto the literary scene. Writers such as Caryl Phillips from St Kitts and a remarkable list of female writers such as Edwidge Danticat from Haiti, Cristina García from Cuba, Esmeralda Santiago and Rosario Ferré from Puerto Rico emerged in France, Canada and the USA. Other writers, such as Édouard Glissant, Antonio Benítez-Rojo from Cuba, Emile Ollivier from Haiti, Olive Senior from Jamaica and I, for reasons of our own, seem to have chosen exile. The referential context in our works of fiction represents other places. Characters are as diverse as their referential environment. Sometimes, as in the case of Phillips' *Nature of Blood* (1997), the novel's hero is not black but a Jew; and the author dares compare the Middle Passage with the Holocaust. We are far from the time when Jean Metellus shocked the reader by placing the intrigue of his *Une eau forte* (1983) in a Swiss environment.[15] Glissant's

14 See Senghor, *Liberté*, I.

15 See Caryl Phillips, *The Nature of Blood* (New York: Alfred A. Knopf, 1997); Jean Metellus, *Une eau forte* (Paris: Gallimard, 1983).

lyrical treatise on the Creolization of the world is called
Tout-Monde (1993).[16] In my last novel, *Desirada* ([1997]
2000), I described three generations of women: Nina, the
grandmother, who has never left La Désirade, the island
where she was born; Reynalda, the daughter, who emigrates to Paris when the BUMIDOM was in its heyday and
the granddaughter, Marie-Noelle, raised in the dismal con-
finement of the Paris suburbs, who emigrates to the USA
and settles in Boston.[17] All three women illustrate the journeys of the Caribbean people. At first tiny communities
surrounded by the ocean, a collection of isolated islands,
today a people of nomads recreating the land of origin
wherever they can. To be Caribbean or African is no longer
merely a question of origin, ethnicity, language or colour.
The main contribution of the Second Generation writers
is having eliminated the binary opposition between out-
siders and insiders and colonial language versus mother
tongue which rages in the Third World. Until recently, the
essentialism of language was a creed—like that of Race.
Everyone had in mind the famous phrase of the Bishop of
Avila to Queen Isabella of Spain: 'Language is the perfect
instrument of empire.' It was commonplace to believe
that a language contained a specific vision of the world,
and consequently, to impose a language on an individual
or a people resulted in great trauma. It was Bakhtin who
introduced the theory of hybridization of languages, 'a
mixture of two social languages within the limits of a single utterance [. . .] between two different linguistic con-
sciousnesses, separated from one another by an epoch, by

16 Édouard Glissant, *Tout-Monde* (Paris: Gallimard, 1993).

17 See Maryse Condé, *Desirada* (Richard Philcox trans.) (New York:
Soho Press, 2000).

social differentiation or by some other factor.'[18] In other words, Bakhtin tells us that all language is polyphonic. Danticat and García deliberately chose to write in English and not in French, Creole or Spanish, and illustrate this hybridization, this polyphony and power of any language to model itself on ethnicity, personal history and gender. At the same time, they put an end to the debate on a novel's authenticity. For some in the French Antilles, the language of authenticity is Creole. One of the criticisms aimed at Césaire refers to his real or supposed contempt for Creole. Likewise, Kenyan Ngũgĩ wa Thiong'o recommends [in 1976] abandoning English and using African languages. Is it worth pursuing this debate? What is the meaning of the word 'authentic'? There is no such thing as authentic fiction since fiction is nothing but the representation of the world by an isolated individual. Or perhaps every fiction is authentic since it translates the complexity of the self.

Even more seriously, our female novelists challenge the very nature of identity: What becomes of it when you take away the solid foundations of language, skin colour and origin? Isn't it simply a matter of choice dictated by a number of subjective values, such as the image and role of women, the relationship to the invisible, and the notion of death?

I am fully conscious of certain objections. The globalization of the Third Millenium for the moment has nothing in common with the dreams of the black intellectuals

18 Mikhail M. Bakhtin, 'Discourse in the Novel' in *The Dialogic Imagination: Four Essays* (Michael Holquist ed., Caryl Emerson and Michael Holquist trans) (Austin: University of Texas Press, 1981), pp. 259–422; here, p. 358.

at the beginning of the twentieth century. It is not the elimination of prejudice and complexes as the world's borders expand. It will, rather, be the confrontation between the technologically advanced countries and the least developed ones. It will be the imposition of the formers' values or non-values on the latter and the rout of the weak who will not be able to safeguard their culture.

Nevertheless, the face of Africa is imperceptibly changing and, as Malcolm X once said: 'If the face of Africa changes, the condition of the Negroes throughout the world will change.' Despite terrible difficulties, new powers are emerging in Central Africa, Mozambique and South Africa. Even in West Africa, regimes are less dictatorial. Martinique, in the French Antilles, the bastion of colonialism, has elected its first member of Parliament from the independence movement. Provided we know how to work it, globalization will perhaps mean the advent of a more open world where the notions of race, nationality and language, which have long divided us, can be defined otherwise while the concepts of hybridization and *métissage* will take on new meaning. Perhaps globalization is the cartography of Shakespeare's *Tempest*. I am not so naive as to believe that all our problems will disappear and that, in the words of John Lennon, 'the world will be one.' But I am convinced that with the help of our artists and intellectuals and aided by a different generation of politicians, we will manage to overcome the challenges of the future.

Literature and Globalization

The following reflection on the consequences of globalization as a political factor on literature goes back many years.

One event in particular comes to mind. In 2004, I was
commissioned by the regional authorities of Guadeloupe
to organize a colloquium celebrating the first arrival of the
East Indians to our island. They arrived on board the
Aurélie, now a mythical vessel in the Indian consciousness,
unlike the first slave ship whose name has not been kept
by the African descendants. We know that the Indians were
shipped to Guadeloupe and Martinique to replace the
African slaves. Since the slaves no longer wanted to culti-
vate the land after the abolition of slavery in 1848, they
abandoned the sugar plantations, leaving the islands' economy threatened with ruin.

The colloquium's participants included notable international personalities, such as Professor Gayatri Chakravorty Spivak and Mauritian writer Ananda Devi. Among
the French contingent was well-known ethnologist Professor Jean Benoîst, specialist of the Caribbean and responsible
for the remarkable *L'Archipel inachevé*.[1] On concluding his
presentation, however, he was sharply taken to task by a

Presented at Oriel College, Oxford, September 2010.

1 See Jean Benoîst (ed.), *L'Archipel inachevé: culture et société aux Antilles
Françaises* (Montreal: Les Presses de l'Université de Montreal, 1972).

group of Caribbean researchers, including Michael Dash from Trinidad and Gerry Létang from Martinique. Benoîst insisted that the Indians were voluntary immigrants. They had enrolled as indentured labourers for 36 months to work in the sugarcane fields. Although very few managed to do so, they were free to return home at the end of their contract. According to Benoîst, this possibility of a return to their native land configured their imagination differently.

While acknowledging the validity of his remark, Caribbean researchers asked whether this notion of 'voluntary immigration' might not be considered a simplistic argument. If an individual is unable to find work at home, which was the case of the Indians, is unable to feed or take care of his family and is consequently forced to brave the oceans and exile in a foreign land, can we really talk about a choice or a decision to immigrate voluntarily? The discussion was heated and remained inconclusive.

In their defence, it is obvious that the Caribbean researchers were thinking of the miserable condition of their own people. The Caribbean region has never known full employment and has always been a place of poverty and immigration that we could hardly call 'voluntary'. In 1934, for instance, the Panama Canal was dug by both English- and French-speaking hands. In her book *Small Island* (2004), Andrea Levy recalls the massive exodus of Jamaicans after the Second World War.[2] In order to compensate for the shortage of labour after the end of the war in Algeria, the French created the BUMIDOM in 1960 which skimmed off the unemployed in Guadeloupe and Martinique.

It is estimated today that there are 800,000 people from the overseas departments residing in France, mainly

2 Andrea Levy, *Small Island* (New York: Picador, 2005).

in the Paris area, i.e. more than the population of the two islands combined.[3] Sociologists term metropolitan France the 'fifth department'. Although the children born on French soil from this wave of immigration—the Second Generations—are treated with less hostility than the Muslim North Africans, their future prospects are dim. They were targeted at a recent national congress on French identity, accused of being polluters and ordered to integrate. For many Caribbean researchers, then, can the globalization we are witnessing today be considered a mere avatar of slavery, an extension to the entire planet of the fate once reserved for Africans alone and resulting in 'disposable people' worldwide? I had no qualms saying so.

In 2001, I was appointed President, Committee for the Memory of Slavery by French president Jacques Chirac. This committee had been created after the enactment of the Taubira law in France, the first country to recognize slavery as a crime against humanity. This position conferred a certain visibility on my acts and words. A number of French intellectuals, however, did not appreciate my stand on what I called the first and second globalizations. In their opinion, this parallel between the dual systems of slavery and globalization was meaningless. The former was based on punishment, torture and coercion whereas the latter did not involve any form of violence. No form of violence? I gave considerable thought to such a claim.

When the Haitian boat people, sighted off the shores of Florida by the American coastguard, threw themselves overboard and drowned in great numbers, hadn't they undergone an ultimate form of violence? When the anger

3 See Alain Anselin, *Emigration antillaise en France* (Paris: Karthala, 1990).

of the young immigrants cooped up in their housing projects set the Paris suburbs alight, wasn't that a form of violence? And the same goes for when the French police chased two teenagers, one from North Africa, the other from sub-Saharan Africa, and forced them to hide in an electrical transformer where they were electrocuted. I was convinced that globalization too was a form of violence, even though it did not involve brutality on board the slave ships, branding, whipping or mutilation in the horror of the plantation. Nevertheless, these critics goaded me on in my reflection. I accepted the principle whereby no system implies Absolute Evil. Despite its brutality, despite everything, out of slavery emerged the rich and complex cultures of the Caribbean. I began, therefore, to search for I dare not say the beneficial effects but at least the possible positive aspects generated by globalization. To my surprise, there was no lack of them and I discovered a number of important factors to qualify my initial approach.

First of all, globalization has delivered us from the terrorism of language. For years in the French Antilles, French and Creole waged a merciless war. Those who wrote in Creole, the language forged by the slaves and born in the plantation system, were considered close to the people and the authentic children of the island. Those who wrote in French, the language of colonization, were traitors, at best, alienated. Césaire, himself, the founder of Antillean literature, was practically declared an outlaw by the Créolité writers, especially by Confiant.[4] The fact that writers of Haitian origin transplanted at a young age in the USA like Danticat and Chancy manage to express their Caribbean-

---

4 See Raphaël Confiant, *Aimé Césaire: Une traversée paradoxale du siècle* (Paris: Stock, 1993).

ness in English in such a talented way dealt a serious blow
to the signifying hegemony of Creole. Subsequently, Díaz
from the Dominican Republic in his *Brief Wondrous Life of
Oscar Wao* created and imposed his own half-English, half-
Spanish idiom on his disconcerted readers. Thanks to these
striking examples I came to understand that language is
the first and primordial space of the writer's freedom. No
one has the right to dictate to him his options and I can
finally say: 'I write neither in French nor in Creole. I write
in Maryse Condé.'

By dispersing people haphazardly and forcing them to
meet and communicate, globalization has dealt a serious
blow to the notions of belonging and origin and, especially,
identity. The daughter of Jamaican parents, born in the UK,
Zadie Smith, author of *White Teeth* (2000), recognizes that
the place of birth is no longer the fruit of chance.[5] As a
result, we may very well ask ourselves: If countries become
a patchwork of immigrants, is there still such a thing as
collective identity? Isn't identity a singular story formed by
individual experience? What is the identity of a Second
Generation born in Sarcelles, France, who has only seen
the Antilles while on holiday? However hard his parents
strive to make him behave like a Guadeloupean, he can't.
Is he then a fully-fledged Frenchman? The answer to this
question abounds in consequences. The racist and xeno-
phobic society in which he lives does not allow him to
become one.

Globalization has also produced the worldwide
phenomenon of world music (for want of a better term).
The 'Kassav' group, comprising Martinicans and Guadeloupeans, born in exile, which burst onto the music scene in

5 See Zadie Smith, *White Teeth* (New York: Penguin, 2000).

the 1990s, has introduced a new and unique sound which only faintly echoes the traditional music of the islands. We should also mention all the Haitian groups who grew up in New York, performing in English or Creole, whose rhythms are clearly different from, for example, the classical meringue.

The phenomenon is not only musical as was long believed. Globalization has engendered new literary forms. Are these new writers from the Paris suburbs the heirs of those North Africans living in France who were so successful these past years? Faiza Guène and Rachid Djaidani, to name but two, have not received the attention they deserve and, for obvious reasons, remain marginalized.

I now think it interesting to try and see how globalization has progressively affected my work. For this brief analysis, I have selected three books.

The first is *Segu* published in 1984, the second *Desirada* published in 1997 and the third and last is *En attendant la montée des eaux* (Waiting for the Waters to Rise) published in 2010.

Segu narrated the story of a noble family, the Traorés, who lived in the powerful Bambara kingdom of Segu. They were proud of their social rank, origin and ethnicity. Here I describe polygamy (feminists criticized me for not writing pages against female excision), the relations between men and women, the status and role of women, the condition of domestic slaves and the importance of religion, animist or fetishist. I was without a doubt paying homage to African grandeur. *Segu*, however, was different from Alex Haley's *Roots* since it cast a critical look at the African past, discreetly underscoring the internal and external causes for what we must call the decadence of a continent. Such is the meaning of the Bambara words inscribed as an epigraph: 'Segu is a garden where cunning grows. Segu is built on treachery. Speak of Segu outside Segu, but do not speak of Segu in Segu.'[6]

Despite these reservations, *Segu* was seen as a book written by a devout disciple of Césaire, imbued with the values of Negritude and convinced that technical superiority does not imply spiritual and cultural superiority.

The tone changes in *Desirada*. Gone are the vast courtyards, the centuries-old dubale trees and the noble trappings. The heroine, Marie-Noëlle, born of an immigrant Guadeloupean mother, grows up in the low-cost housing estates of Savigny sur Orge in the Paris suburbs. She travels a lot, marries a Jamaican musician who has never been to Jamaica and ends up in Boston where she becomes a university teacher. The book is a study of the complex relations between mother and daughter. The intrigue revolves round Marie-Noëlle's obsession to know who her father is. After having believed her mother's so-called confession, she ends up wondering whether her story was not pure fiction. But the effects of globalization gradually put her in touch with individuals as incomplete and imperfect as herself, swept along by migration and exile, and she finally realizes that to know one's origin and family tree is not paramount and that she must live as she is, by assuming her shortcomings and failures.

En attendant la montée des eaux takes us back to Segu. The main character, Babakar, is one of the last of the famous Traorés. He is of mixed blood since his mother is Guadeloupean. He does not live in Segu but in a country where this Bambara identity of which his ancestors were

6 Condé, *Segu*, p. 3.

so proud, poses a problem. He is taken for a 'Northerner' since he is Muslim. He is dragged into a civil war which is beyond his understanding. Finally he ends up in Haiti, a place for living dangerously. The book is composed of three parallel stories: that of Babakar; that of Movar, the young Haitian; and that of Fouad, the Palestinian, all of whom maintain close ties. All three discover that their lives are variants of a similar schema, tossed round by violence and constantly subjected to exclusion. The lesson of the novel is that in this world without markers, borders or points of reference, our only refuge is friendship, affection and love, not between individuals with the same origin and identity but, on the contrary, between individuals whose only common factor is that they belong to the human species.

It therefore appears evident that globalization has, unknowingly, affected the themes of my novels. It is more difficult to say whether it has entailed other transformations, such as modifying the novel's structure and narrative technique. It is true that the omniscient narrator is dying; that the polyphonic novel written with alternate voices is growing in numbers. But can we definitely say that this is a consequence of globalization? Isn't it rather a sign of the times stamped by the knowledge experienced from psychoanalysis and by the fact that everything is relative?

To conclude, everyone knows John Lennon's song 'Imagine' (1971):

Imagine there're no countries
It isn't hard to do
Nothing to live or die for
And no religion too
Imagine all the people

Living life in peace
You may say I'm a dreamer
But I'm not the only one
I hope someday you will join us
And the world will be as one.

Is globalization one step along the road to John Lennon's dream?

A Servant to Two Masters

CÉSAIRE AND FANON

I have often told the story of how the discovery of Césaire changed the course of my life. Emerging from a tranquil and uneventful childhood and adolescence I thought little about questioning my identity. Raised by parents for whom France was truly the mother country and not the seat of some colonial power, I considered myself to be French. For me, the colour of my skin was of little importance. It was certainly not a sign of inferiority but the result of a series of historical coincidences. In Paris, I took for granted that I had to prepare for the competitive entrance exams to France's elite schools and docilely obeyed the rigours of the Lycée Fénelon. It was there that a classmate and fellow candidate, daughter of a famous Marxist historian who taught at the Sorbonne, handed me a book by a Martinican poet. 'Have you read that?'

It was *The Notebook of a Return to My Native Land*. Although I was so fond of poetry I had never heard of it. I shall always remember the following night, a genuine mystic revelation of that Negritude I didn't know I possessed.

> my negritude is not a stone, its deafness hurled
> against the clamour of the day

Originally published as 'Servir deux maîtres' in Annick Thébia Melsan (ed.), *Aimé Césaire, Le Legs* (Paris: Argol, 2009), pp. 118–22.

> my negritude is not an opaque spot of dead water
> over the dead eye of the earth
> my negritude is neither a tower nor a cathedral
> it reaches deep down into the red flesh of the soil
> it reaches deep into the blazing flesh of the sky
> it pierces opaque prostration with its straight
> patience.[1]

I wasn't content, however, with this simple lyrical effervescence and the very next day I bought and read everything that Césaire had published, especially *Discourse on Colonialism* ([1955] 1972)which became the bedside book that radically transformed me.[2] From an ordinary French girl I became a colonized subject determined to decolonize myself. I also read the Negritude poets, such as Jacques Roumain, David Diop, Léon Laleau and Léopold Sédar Senghor. With the iconoclastic enthusiasm of the newly converted, I questioned all my values. Wherever possible, I abandoned everything I had striven for and made a clean sweep of what I had wanted to be. To say therefore that Césaire is responsible for my political commitment as well as my passion for Africa is no exaggeration.

'Africa, you are in me like the splinter in the wound.'[3]

A few years later I arrived in Conakry on the arm of a Guinean husband, determined to be born again. To my

---

1 Césaire, *Notebook*, p. 115.

2 Aimé Césaire, *Discours sur le colonialisme* (Paris: Presence Africaine, 1955). Available in English as: *Discourse on Colonialism* (Joan Pinkham trans.) (New York: Monthly Review Press, 1972).

3 Jacques Roumain, 'Bois-d'ébène' (1945) in Léopold Sédar Senghor, *Anthologie de la nouvelle poésie nègre et malgache* (Paris: Presses universitaires de France, 1948), p. 116. Also cited in Sartre, 'Black Orpheus', *The Aftermath of War*, p. 320 (translation modified).

amazement, this country of the revolution had been drained to the last drop and devastated. Despite my inexperience, I dare not say my naivety, my faith in Negritude was on the verge of collapse. It was obvious that the population was groaning under the boot of a black power as ferocious as the previous white one. While the children were dying like flies from measles and other benign illnesses in a neglected, run-down hospital and the adults, who could, crowded through the gates of exile, shortly after my arrival, the government, who was not wanting for contradictions, decreed a week's national mourning in honour of Fanon who had just passed away in Bethesda. Unlike Césaire's, I had long been familiar with the name of Fanon. When a favourable review of his book *Black Skin, White Masks* was published in the journal *Esprit*, I signed a letter on behalf of all my girlfriends who lived like me in the bourgeois student residence on the rue Lhomond, in which we 'the young people from Guadeloupe and Martinique' objected to the false and vicious representation of the population from our islands.[4] Lactification complex? Not at all! This unexpected national mourning in a country muzzled by dictatorship was an opportunity for me to immerse myself in Fanon's work of which I knew nothing except *Black Skin, White Masks*. Against all expectations, I was completely transformed once again. How could I have gone on living without it? In *The Wretched of the Earth*, I read and reread the chapters on national culture and the trials and tribulations of national consciousness. I had the strange impression that Fanon was targeting the Guinean authorities: 'Instead of being the

4 See Maxime Chastaing, 'Frantz Fanon: *Peau noire, masques blancs*', *Esprit* 20(195) (October 1952): 556–9.

coordinated crystallization of the people's innermost aspirations, instead of being the most tangible, immediate
product of popular mobilization, national consciousness
is nothing but a crude, empty, fragile shell.'[5]

From that moment on I had two mentors; I analysed
every sentence, I weighed every word and never stopped
wavering between the two. Oddly enough, despite his
numerous attacks on Negritude and his gibes at the 'bard'
as he liked to call him, Fanon never eliminated Césaire. On
account of his generation and the particularities of his
struggle, Fanon simply dares to go further. The picture of
Martinique which emerges from their texts is the same—
a pitiful and pathetic people, 'the only undeniable record
we ever broke was endurance under the whip'.[6] Yet the
solutions they recommend for remedying the situation dif-
fer considerably. For Césaire, the spiritual return to African
values is imperative. For Fanon, it is the armed struggle
that will forge a new man. Fanon is conscious of a reality
which his elder has always denied—colonialism has ruined
Africa and plundered and destroyed its cultures and so-
called 'spirituality'. All things considered, both men are by
no means radically opposed, as we might first think. I soon
realized that, on the contrary, they complement each other.
Césaire's most inflammatory text, *Discourse on Colonialism*,
as well as some of his angry and rebellious pages from
Notebook could have been written by a young Fanon at the
dawn of his career as rebel and martyr. Strangely, Césaire
seems to have intuition of Fanon's major theory where
revolutionary violence responds to colonial violence and
it alone can liberate the colonized. In *And the Dogs Were*

5 Fanon, *The Wretched of the Earth*, p. 97.

6 Césaire, *Notebook*, p. 105.

Silent, once the rebel has killed his master and received his blood full in the face, he declares: 'It is the only baptism that today I remember.'[7]

Unfortunately he doesn't take it any further, doesn't elaborate on it and writes this capital line as if it were incidental.

The style of both writers is also magnificent, imbued with the same telluric fervour, issued from the same soil.

In 1962, the so-called teachers' plot allowed Sékou Touré to jail the last real or false opponents. Many students, mostly children, perished. The Boiro concentration camp loomed large on the horizon. On leaving the country I buried my last hopes in Negritude. Yes, I was now convinced that race was a signifier that signified nothing. The black people were close to one another, identical even, only when they were captured by the white gaze. A black leader could remorselessly oppress and kill black people if profit required it. Perhaps the members of the black power movement who raised their fists in the USA were nothing more than apprentice dictators! What a pity they never had time to prove themselves.

And yet I never managed completely to liberate myself from Negritude. My entire work is a balancing act between two extremes. For example, in the early 1980s, I travelled to Mali and the outcome was *Segu*, whose inspiration came entirely from Césaire. I was infused with the beauty and power of the African past whose pulse I felt for the first time in that region. Although the book openly aims for a certain objectivity, and in doing so shocked quite a few, it does cover up a number of flaws.

7 Aimé Césaire, *And the Dogs Were Silent* in *Lyric and Dramatic Poetry*, p. 41.

To conclude, I would say that I have not established a hierarchy between my two masters, Aimé Césaire and Frantz Fanon. I do not seek to know who is the more gifted or the more important in our literary pantheon. Nor what is the value of their legacy. This Negritude that I so contested in the past now seems to me to be the last magnificent dream for our humanity—a generous dream of brotherhood where the blackness of our skins ties us to each other like the vine of the yam; a political dream too where the barriers between our countries would fall and migration would be nothing more than a visit.

What have we replaced it by in this era of disunion?

Kréyol Factory

> *The factory would be a place of healing: hybrid and vector of hybridity, origin and cause.*

Valérie John, Martinican artist.

In these times when Francophony has high ambitions and claims to commit hara-kiri, all the better to tackle the entire world, the title of this exhibition is a pleasant surprise.

Kréyol Factory!

Two words, foreign sounding. The first belongs to that language, once considered gibberish, which a generation of militant linguists strived to rehabilitate and impose on the recalcitrant and half-hearted. At first reserved for only the white elements of the population in a social system where the European planters dominated a slave labour of African origin, the term gradually spread to include every member of society before being claimed by some as a definition of identity. In *In Praise of Creoleness*, Martinicans Bernabé, Chamoiseau and Confiant declared in French:

Preface to the exhibition catalogue *Kréyol Factory: Des artistes interrogent les identités créoles* (Paris: Gallimard, 2009), pp. 14–21. The exhibition *Kréyol Factory* was on view between 7 April and 5 July 2009 at the Grande Halle de la Villette, Paris.

'Neither Amerindian, nor European, African nor Asian, we proclaim ourselves Creoles.'[1]

The second word is not even a mixture of French and English, which we could partly forgive. It is well and truly English. The dictionary gives us the following definition for factory: A building or group of buildings in which goods are manufactured or assembled. Kréyol Factory, therefore, is a place for producing Creole cultural products. This unusual title, which proclaims its alterity, also indicates the total freedom of choice for an exhibit which endeavours to be singular. On second thought, it is just as clear as a 'For Sale' sign in front of a house. By a series of semantic shifts, Kréyol Factory means, in other words, 'Regions of Creole Culture'. It straightaway implies that the exhibition is resolutely anchored in the here and now. It illustrates what is currently produced in certain regions which are grouped according to their surprising similarities or, on the contrary, their glaring dissimilarities, and are never defined, as is usually the case, solely in relation to their origin or past or the influence of their *métropoles*, which in many cases have long ceased to exist.

The exhibition *Kréyol Factory* resolutely speaks in the present tense and assembles a whole range of artistic creations which are especially precious since, before coming to fruition on their own, for all to see and analyse, they are the result of painful parturitions. Neither heavily pedagogical nor didactic, its main aim is to highlight the aesthetic, although the signifier is never neglected. In short, far from encouraging a certain artistic voyeurism, its aim is to get those who have two eyes to see, to think. Some people,

1 Bernabé, Chamoiseau and Confiant, 'In Praise of Creoleness', p. 886.

however, will soon object that this apparently appealing and illuminating title risks being seen as restrictive. Doesn't it appear to isolate from the rest of the world those regions included in the exhibition? Doesn't it transform them into case studies or individual cases? And consequently, might not the visitor be forced to think that Creolization is a characteristic particular to certain societies, victims of colonial violence, whether they are now overseas departments or independent countries?

Such an interpretation would be hasty and erroneous. It would not take into account the content of the exhibition. For example, in a striking prologue, two female artists from two regions as different as South Africa and black America, give us their amazingly convergent visions despite the apparent effects of alienation in which their peoples live.

It is a well-known fact that the words Kréyol or Creole cover a wide range of meaning without distinction of geography. Quite rightly, Jack Beng-Thi, the artist from La Réunion, warns us mysteriously that 'the purpose of geography is primarily to make love'![2] This awareness of the self's and society's cultural multiplicity, originally a mass of contradictory components, is nothing new, although it has increased meaning today. In France, it goes back at least to Michel de Montaigne when he boasts of the merits of the honest man with the manner of a universal man. It found its apogee in Brazil at the beginning of the twentieth century with Oswald and Mário de Andrade, the two leaders of the Modernist Movement. By rehabilitating the Tupi Indians, considered by the Catholic church of Portugal to

2 The title of one of his works from 1998. See *Kréyol Factory* catalogue, p. 46.

be the very incarnation of barbarism because of their unfortunate custom of eating missionaries in order to appropriate their virtues, they laid the foundation of national culture in its plurality. Oswald de Andrade wrote *Manifesto Antropofagò* in 1928, an inspired, theoretical hoax, where he mockingly cannibalized Shakespeare's *Hamlet* and, through him, all the European values which had unconsciously influenced him.[3]

The pastiche, touchstone line of the *Manifesto* goes as follows: 'Tupi or not Tupi, that is the question.'[4]

Mário de Andrade wrote the wonderfully lavish novel *Macunaíma* in 1929, the uncontested masterpiece of Brazilian literature, who liked to repeat on a more serious note than his counterpart: 'I am a Tupi who plays the lute.'[5]

The idea that cultures are watertight and possibly organized into a hierarchy as well as beliefs in the resulting notions of purity and authenticity has slowly but surely collapsed. In fact, such an idea can be dangerously abused. It has been acknowledged that whenever societies come into contact, be it by force, such as slavery, colonization and neo-colonization, or more peacefully, such as today's rural exodus and migration, they embark upon a process of common transformation, which is to say, creolization. As far back as 1971, Barbadian writer Edward Kamau

3 First published in *Revista de Antropofagia* 1 (May 1928): 3–7. Translated into English by Leslie Bary as 'Cannibalist Manifesto', *Latin American Literary Review* 19(38) (July–December 1991): 35–47.

4 Andrade, 'Cannibalist Manifesto', p. 38.

5 Mário de Andrade, *Macunaíma* (E. A. Goodland trans.) (New York: Random House, 1984). The line is from Andrade's *Hallucinated City* [1922] (Jack E. Tomlins trans.) (Nashville, TN: Vanderbilt University Press, 1968), pp. 22–3.

Braithwaite demonstrated it with regard to Jamaica in his now classic *The Development of Creole Society in Jamaica, 1770–1820*.[6] This process, which has always existed, has accelerated and been amplified today by globalization.

In *The Tale Tellers: A Short Study of Humankind* (2008), a book that is both deeply serious and hilarious, Nancy Huston reminds us that she's a mixture like everyone else. Her ancestors came to Canada from just about everywhere in Europe, from countries who were enemies, Scotland and Ireland, England and Germany.[7]

All hybrids, mestizos, mixed bloods, half-castes, Kréyols, Creoles. Choose the term you like! All united against the Bastilles of univocal societies! The world is a gigantic Kréyol Factory, no one should forget it any longer.

So although the 'Discoverers' wearing helmets and boots planted their standards in the gold of the Caribbean beaches before rushing back on board their caravels, and hence did not have time to become Kréyol, the slaves—who, according to Guadeloupean novelist Daniel Maximin, performed rituals round the 'tree of oblivion' in order to prepare for life in the hell of the plantations by mutilating their memory—were also preparing for a future transformation of their being in the most frightful way.[8]

The exhibition *Kréyol Factory* is divided into seven segments, scanning a range of Creole worlds. They have been given somewhat enigmatic and poetical names which

6 See Edward Kamau Braithwaite, *The Development of Creole Society in Jamaica, 1770–1820* (Oxford: Clarendon Press, 1971).

7 See Nancy Huston, *The Tale Tellers: A Short Study of Humankind* (Toronto: McArthur & Company, 2008).

8 See Daniel Maximin, *Tu, c'est l'enfance* (Paris: Gallimard, 2008).

arouse our curiosity: Crossings, Troubling Appearances, Africa in the Imagination, How to Be Black? Islands Under the Influence, the New Worlds and At Home Far Away. Each segment is punctuated with texts, quotations, information, citations by artists and above all extracts from documentaries and documents which we know are especially conducive to historical analysis.

But I have no intention of doing the work for you, guiding you by the hand and explaining every detail, word by word. Follow me, if you like. I shall stroll along at my own pace, stopping at random to meditate, criticize or question or even walk through some of the rooms without stopping.

After the prologue, the exhibition well and truly opens with two paintings by Guadeloupean painter Thierry Alet, reproducing pages, inscriptions like the Ten Commandments we could say, from Césaire's *Notebook of a Return to My Native Land*, a magical and prophetic text which revealed to generations both the reality of themselves as well as the false constructions of the world round them. Césaire is the founding father and the most accomplished son of our literature. I maintain, however, that he will not go down in history for his theory of Negritude, much debated and constantly contradicted by reality, although he never abandoned it as witnessed by his last conversation with Francoise Verges in *Nègre je suis, Nègre je resterai* (2005).[9] He will shine for eternity because of the magnificently lyrical power of his revolt and his painful irony:

> As there are hyena-men and panther-men, I shall
> be a Jew-man

9 See Aimé Césaire and Francoise Verges, *Nègre je suis, Nègre je resterai* (Paris: Albin Michel, 2005).

a kaffir-man
a Hindu-from-Calcutta-man
a man-from-Harlem-who-does-not-vote
the starvation-man, the insult-man, the torture-
man, one could grab him at any time, beat him
up, kill him—yes, kill him too—without having
to account to anyone, without having to apolo-
gize to anyone
a Jew-man
a pogrom-man
a puppy,
a beggar
but who can kill Remorse beautiful as the stupe-
fied face of an English lady finding a Hottentot's
skull in her soup-tureen?[10]

The exhibition closes again well and truly with a quote from Fanon, the rebel who turned his back on his native Martinique and chose to inseminate the soil of Algeria. It is thus book-ended between two masters, carried by their voices which echo each other in harmony.

Certain segments of the exhibition attract our attention in particular.

'Africa,' wrote Haitian Jacques Roumain, 'You are in me like the splinter in the wound.'[11]

The third segment is devoted to Africa in the Imagi-nation and appeals directly to our obsessions. Haiti imme-diately comes to mind, as does Jamaica, since we too often forget that, like voodoo, Rastafarianism is a dream of Africa even though it is not rooted in the mangroves of

---

10 Césaire, *Notebook*, pp. 85–7.

11 Cited in Sartre, 'Black Orpheus', *The Aftermath of War*, p. 320.

Benin or the Middle Passage. This is an innovating segment since the profane is mixed with the sacred, i.e. carnival shows up alongside Rastafarianism and voodoo. All things considered, such a mixture has nothing sacrilegious about it. With due respect, voodoo does often bear a familiar resemblance to carnival. Inside the voodoo *houmforts*, the reds of the unfolded flags dominate. The drums resonate. The reeling steps of the possessed resemble those of the carnival dancers. In fact, in a subtle kind of way, carnival, Rastafarianism and voodoo all revolve round the floats of Desperation and Death. Haitian painter André Pierre attracts our attention with his voluptuous and sinister forms representing Ezili Danto and Baron de Mer while sculptor Louis Juste tortures metal to revive the sinister familiar silhouettes of Baron Lacroix and Baron Samedi whose other name was perhaps Papa Doc. These complex shapes and pictures irresistibly bring to mind an extract from the novel *Pays sans chapeau* (1996) by Haitian writer Dany Laferrière where despair, humour and madness cavalcade hand in hand:

'The country has changed, my friend. The people you pass in the street are not all human beings.'

'Why do you say that? What about yourself?'

'Me? (He laughs). Me! I've been dead for a long time. I'm going to tell you a secret about this country. All those people you see walking or talking in the street, well, most of them died a long time ago and they don't know it. This country has become the biggest graveyard in the world.'[12]

---

12 Dany Laferrière, *Pays sans chapeau* (Paris: Le Serpent à plumes, 1999), p. 56.

No need for a scholarly transition to begin the next segment. Let us stop at one of its subheadings: One Island, the Other Haiti / Dominican Republic which shows us a different face of Haiti, a face devoid of mysticism and symbolism. The island of Hispaniola is a she-wolf which suckled the twin enemies of Romulus and Remus. Researcher Jean-Marie Théodat traces the causes of this hatred to the rivalry between the empires of France and Spain in their greed to possess the entire island.[13] Then at the beginning of the nineteenth century, the victorious revolution led by the 'brocaded Africans' (the expression is Napoleon Bonaparte's) and the ensuing massacre of the white planters (*Coupé têt, brilé kaye*—cut off heads and burn the houses— was the watchword) frightened the Dominican Republic which considered its neighbour a dangerous savage, ready to pounce on its territory. Today, there is not only the old antagonism but also a very modern type of ostracism born out of the exploitation of thousands of black Haitian workers. The difficult relations between both sides of the island have resulted in a great many films, novels and paintings. Through the ages, Haitian writers as different as Alexis and Danticat have given us their vision of the same cane cutters' massacre in *General Sun, My Brother* and *The Farming of Bones* (1998) respectively.[14] In this quarrel, our sympathies go out to Haiti. Although we have caricatured the Dominican Republic with the rags of the capitalist oppressor, we tend to forget that it too has experienced dictatorships and tribulations, as Llosa reminds us in *The Feast of the Goat* and Díaz in his *Brief Wondrous Life of Oscar Wao*.

13 See *Kréyol Factory* catalogue, p. 74.

14 Edwidge Danticat, *The Farming of Bones* (New York: Soho Press, 1998).

Its population lives in dire poverty and migrates to the USA where it then undergoes exclusion. The reason for our sympathy is that we have trouble coming to terms with the fact that the descendants of the rebellious slaves, who were the first to plant the tree of liberty, are despised because of their colour and who go down as a few pages in history. The root of the problem lies with the fact that the Dominican Republic and Haiti have both constructed their national discourse and official history on a myth. The former likes to think it is neither African nor Creole and claims the Amerindian as its ancestor. The latter glorifies the Maroon, the runaway slave who has gone back to the bosom of Mother Africa. Two irreconcilable myths.

And here we arrive at the segment Islands under the Influence! We must confess that, at first sight, it seems to be an amusing euphemism for the French overseas departments of the Americas as well as other countries in the region which boast of being independent but are far from it. The entire segment is conducive to reflection; it is rich in interesting artefacts and installations and profound in literary extracts and artists' quotes. With its accompanying videos, these texts and citations eradicate the superficiality and deceiving irony of the title. It is, in fact, openly political. The multiple shapes of dependence are defined—from cultural alienation personified by Empress Josephine standing imposingly in the very centre of the Savane in Fort de France to naked social exploitation. BUMIDOM, created by Michel Debré to compensate for the shortage of labour after the Algerian War (voluntary migration?), was the Beast which, by swallowing so many Antillean men and women and regurgitating the Second Generation, began the dismemberment of Caribbean identity. On closer consideration, the segments Islands Under the Influence and The

New Worlds take us deeper into the meaning and objectives of the exhibition. Underlying the exhibit's contents is the excruciating and agonizing question whose response is yet to be found: What is the role of the artist in these societies constantly struggling against internal demons as well as external factors and subjected to so much suffering? How do they manage to create? Far from being a selfish and elitist act, isn't creation precisely a generous remedy? Let us listen to Valérie John, an artist from Martinique, who in the words of a poet, expresses the painful questioning of the colonized artist:

> The Creole word *Blesse* or traumatism is a specifically Creole illness, triggered by a violent blow or over exertion. They say it is imaginary. Are we stricken with this *blesse* or rather would we like to live with it? Some say they would.
>
> The main thing is to be cured of it [. . .] by every means. Perhaps practicing his art is the artist's medicine [. . .] a kind of obeah man.
>
> The factory would be a place of healing: it would be hybrid and vector of hybridity. It would be origin and cause.[15]

Let us continue our interrogation along the same lines. Can the creation of a single individual help his community to survive? Can the artist achieve Césaire's dream of being: 'My mouth will be the mouth of those griefs which have no mouth'?[16] Is he his people's miracle-worker? Can he forge miraculous weapons for them? Other questions plague us, such as: How important are the components of

15 *Kréyol Factory* catalogue, p. 137.

16 Césaire, *Notebook*, p. 89.

culture in the traditional meaning of the term? 'Culture' is a word we tremble to pronounce since we no longer know exactly what it looks like: globalization oblige, as Martinican painter Ernest Breleur says ironically. We would have to linger over each segment, look at each object, weigh every installation, meditate every artist's words, listen to every recording and play back again and again every video, if need be, with no guarantee of finding an immediate answer, for it is more important to question than to understand.

In the last segment, At Home Far Away, I have noted the words of Zadie Smith in her book *White Teeth*: '[Y]ou begin to give up the *very idea* of belonging. Suddenly, this thing, this *belonging*, it seems like some long, dirty lie . . . and I begin to believe that birthplaces are accidents, that everything is an *accident*.'[17]

These words have enormous repercussions. Until recently, we considered identity a collective phenomenon. It was a uniform we all had to slip on whether we liked it or not. To be Guadeloupean was to be born in Guadeloupe, to have Guadeloupean parents, preferably descended from African slaves, and to reside on the island; to like *zouk* music and mangoes. Our fathers and mothers lived this way, were proud of being born and bred on the island, travelled little and heaped the pejorative nicknames of Negropolitans and Negzagonals on those who had the misfortune of being born and living outside the island paradises. It goes without saying that a perfect knowledge of Creole, the mother tongue, was indispensable. Unemployment and the ensuing massive migration changed the order of things. A fifth overseas department mushroomed

17 Smith, *White Teeth*, p. 407 (emphasis in the original).

in Paris. Thousands of Guadeloupeans are born and live there where the ill wind of necessity carried their parents in order to survive. Some of them cannot speak Creole, others have only imaginary relations with the island. Strange unions abound with strangers from elsewhere. Confronted with these upheavals, a bell tolls. Identity becomes a personal history, which each and every one of us writes and lives as we like, and Zadie Smith speaks with the same tongue as her fellow novelist Jhumpa Lahiri, an Indian writer married to a Greek Uru-guayan and living in Brooklyn, whose latest book *Unaccustomed Earth* (2008) tops the *New York Times* best-seller list.[18]

Should we be saddened by what's in store for us? It is fashionable to lament the effects of globalization which are said to result in global standardization and the advent of the sad term 'world culture'. In his book *From Cannibals to Radicals* (1996), Haitian Roger Célestin quotes sociologist Ulf Hannertz who, without attempting a definition, is content to explain the reasons for its emergence: 'World culture is created through the increasingly interconnectedness of varied local cultures, as well as through the development of cultures without a clear anchorage in any one territory.'[19]

Let us admit that this transformation of the world has not always been negative. It has lifted a good many taboos,

18 Jhumpa Lahiri, *Unaccustomed Earth* (New York: Alfred A. Knopf, 2008).

19 Ulf Hannerz, 'Cosmopolitans and Locals in World Culture' in Mike Featherstone (ed.), *Global Culture: Nationalism, Globalization and Modernity* (London: Sage, 1990), p. 237. Cited in Roger Célestin, *From Cannibals to Radicals: Figures and Limits of Exoticism* (Minneapolis: University of Minnesota Press, 1996), p. 178.

relativized the imposition of ancestry, of the so-called mother tongue, narrow-minded respect for ancestors and obsession with family values and in many respects has guaranteed our freedom. As Césaire laments in his *Notebook*: 'I am of no nationality provided for by the chancelleries.'[20]

We now know how little nationality counts for. Its sole purpose is to issue a passport for crossing borders. Hearts and imagination have no need for it; they travel freely and settle wherever they like. For the artist, that's all that matters.

How can we sum up the visit we have just made through the *Kréyol Factory*? Any choice, any selection is arbitrary. No approach is exhaustive. No gaze, objective. Such as it is, far from being a guide, an inventory or a catalogue, the exhibition is rather a polyphony, a choir song, an ode to the lavish, baroque, unexpected and unbelievable creativity of those who struggle with the only weapons they possess so that their places of residence are not merely stopovers for timorous and hard-up tourists en route for the Club Med.

---

20 Césaire, *Notebook*, p. 107.

Lands of the Atlantic

Art is always the first to announce what is to come.
Festa Journal, Sao Paulo, Brazil, 1927

Lands of the Atlantic. The expression should be of no surprise. The ocean should be considered a link. It does not split the world into islands, continents and subcontinents but unites it in a fistful of waves, seaweed and spray. It is the ocean that traces the contours of the lands it surrounds. It is a formidable magician, authorizing voyages and orchestrating currents and shipwrecks, and in this respect, a patron of the arts.

Examples of its power abound. It is the year 1609 and, under the dual banner of religion and mercantile ambition, the frontiers of the world have shrunk. Led by Sir Thomas Gates and George Summers, a fleet of ships sails from England for the new colony of Virginia in America. Alas, one of the ships gets separated and is shipwrecked off the coast

Published as 'Introduction' to the catalogue for *Latitudes: Terres de l'Atlantique*, 16 December 2004–12 January 2005, Hotel de Ville, Paris. Also published in the catalogue for *Caribbean: Art at the Crossroads of the World*, 2012–13, El Museo del Barrio, Queens Museum of Art and Studio Museum, New York.

of Bermuda. The crew miraculously manages to survive and reach Virginia. Out of these events was born Shakespeare's undisputed masterpiece *The Tempest*. Many years later, in 1816, and many leagues from there, a convoy of French ships were on their way to recapture the colony of Senegal from the English. One of them was a fast, modern frigate called *La Méduse* which hit a sand bank and ran aground. Thirteen days later, a raft was sighted by the brig *Argus*. Of the fifteen survivors, five died. This tragedy gave birth to another masterpiece, the painting of *The Raft of the Medusa* by Théodore Géricault.

In the area of the world which interests us here, the ocean is the true master on board. It was by the ocean that the caravels of the discoverers first came. Then came the ships that carried away the men and women, bartered on the coast of Africa for barrel organs and sedan chairs. Finally, those vessels which returned home, their holds heavy with 'exotic and foreign' cargoes of which François Rabelais speaks in his book *Le Quart Livre* (1552).[1] It is here in the Atlantic that the ocean performs its most spectacular feats. Let us return to the first masterpiece, *The Tempest*.

Influenced by Montaigne's *Essays* (1580), Shakespeare has placed the character of Caliban, anagram for cannibal, in the centre of his play.[2] At that time, the cannibal fired

1 See François Rabelais, *Five Books of the Lives, Heroic Deeds and Sayings of Gargantua and His Son Pantagruel, Book 4* (Thomas Urquhart of Cromarty and Peter Antony Motteux trans) (Derby: Moray Press, 1894). Available at: www.gutenberg.org/files/8169/8169-h /8169-h.htm (last accessed 14 August 2013).

2 See *Essays of Michel de Montaigne* (Charles Cotton trans., William Carew Hazlitt rev.) (New York: Edwin C. Hill, 1910). Available at: oll.libertyfund.org/option=com_staticxt&staticfile=show.php3Ftitle=168 (last accessed 14 August 2013)

the European imagination. On 23 November 1492, during his first voyage, Christopher Columbus had a memorable encounter which he relates in his journal and which went on to be so rich in consequence: 'They said that it [the land, stretching beyond the cape before them, which the Indians on board called *Bohio*] was very large, and that there were people in it who had one eye in their foreheads, and others who were cannibals, and of whom they were much afraid.'[3]

Caniba. Cariba. Cannibals. *Hombres que comian los hombres.* The word is out.

Except for the existence of Saint-Pierre et Miquelon, an eccentric island, perched way to the North, facing Canada, we would be tempted to name these Lands of the Atlantic 'Land of Cannibals'. In fact whether it was Cuba, Haiti, Jamaica, Dominican Republic, Trinidad and Tobago, Martinique or Guadeloupe, this was the common name given to its inhabitants. These syllables, which were to worm their way first into Western semantics, as in Columbus' imagination, were lumped together with the unlikely Cynocephalus, the man with a dog's head coming from far-off times described by Pliny and Isidore of Seville, or with the peoples of the Great Khan, a contemporary of Marco Polo. Then the image gets simpler. The eater of men was to generate an unprecedented artistic surge in drawings, wood engravings, etchings and reproductions by André Thévet, Hans Staden, Theodor de Bry and Sebastien Münster. This deep-seated terror was to vitalize for a long time all forms of artistic creation. We can recall how frightened

3 Christopher Columbus, 'Reports of Bohio: Friday, 23rd of November' in *Journal of Christopher Columbus (During His First Voyage, 1492–93)* (New York: Cambridge University Press, 2010 [1893]), p. 83.

Daniel Defoe's Robinson Crusoe was during his stay on his desert island which came to a climax on discovering Friday's footprint.

In the Lands of the Atlantic, the fortune of the term cannibal was to be so rich that Glissant declared: 'Shakespeare gave us the word, our writers have made it over.'[4]

Yet it is different. More than a thriving allegory, it was to change into a metaphoric rallying cry whose waves rippled across the Atlantic, from South America to the Caribbean islands. Very soon the cannibal stopped being a monster to evangelize and civilize. He was to become the man discovered in the New World who dreams of utopia and projects his imagination into the future. 'We are utopia fully achieved,' Brazilian Oswald de Andrade proudly declared.[5] Andrade, author of 'Cannibalist Manifesto', rehabilitated his ancestors, the Tupinamba Indians, eaters of Catholic priests, and opens his 'Manifesto' with this diabolical declaration: 'Cannibalism alone unites us. Socially. Economically. Philosophically.'[6]

During the Modern Art Week in Sao Paulo in 1922, which inaugurated the modernist movement in Brazil, Oswald and his wife, avant-garde painter Tarsila do Amaral, played a fundamental role. They called upon liberated minds to trumpet the fanfares of the literary revolution. Thanks to them, the cannibalism metaphor was extended to all artists: painters, photographers, designers and sculptors, who must appropriate EVERYTHING to

4 Glissant, *Caribbean Discourse*, p. 262.

5 See Oswald de Andrade, *A marcha das Utopias* (Rio de Janeiro: Serviço de Documentação, Ministério da Educação e Cultura, 1953).

6 Andrade, 'Cannibalist Manifesto', p. 38.

nurture their work. The barrier erected by the conformists between what was commonly called 'the disciplines' as well as noble and other materials broke down. Wire, plastic bags, old clothes—the cannibal artist was to use every available material.

The story of these Lands of the Atlantic is, oddly enough, punctuated by voyages with no colonial connotation which each time impact the fate of the arts, embody the sacred marriage of artistic forms recommended by Oswald and Tarsila and reconfigure art itself.

In 1943, while Europe was tearing itself apart, André Breton arrived in the Antilles hard on the heels of Cuban painter Wilfredo Lam. Like Columbus before him, he named the places and men, but he named them Surrealists. We must emphasize the fact that Breton was not setting foot on the same soil as Columbus. He did not think of this New World in terms of empire to be conquered and plundered: gold, sugarcane and Eucharist. But in terms of the Other World, embedded like a fertile seed in the heart of his unconscious and capable of nurturing his imagination. In this Other World, the Past meets up with the Future; reality and dreams, pleasures and festivities merge. We can never say enough that Surrealism was meant to be a global movement. Besides Lam, who, thanks to the Surrealists, will realize the full extent of his African roots, the movement included painters Marcel Duchamp, Salvador Dali, André Masson, Roberto Massa and Pablo Picasso himself, to name only a few, as well as photographer Man Ray and sculptor Giacometti. In fact, cannibalism and Surrealism are brothers. They share the same requirements and ambitions. They affirm the superiority of the New or Other World over the Old, petrified in its fears and rancour. Both praise the Absurd (Erasmus' *Praise of Folly*), the magical and the marvellous: 'Let us not mince words,' declared Breton. 'The marvelous is always beautiful, anything marvelous is beautiful; in fact only the marvelous is beautiful.'[7]

We may be right in thinking that the seeds went out from here to nourish the Haitian theory of 'marvellous realism' dear to René Depestre and Jacques Stephen Alexis and foster entire areas of artistic production. Finally, Surrealism and cannibalism advocate the urgency for a 'luminous poetical frenzy' (Arthur Rimbaud's disordering of the senses?) which implies the questioning of conventions. Together with a violent affinity for provocation and hoaxes, they both reject Order which can result in rebellion and prove finally to be political.

We should also include among these voyages of give and take Paul Gauguin's voyage to Martinique. Gauguin was strongly influenced by his mother's Peruvian (cannibal?) heritage and sought further inspiration in other climes. And, above all, André Malraux's voyage to Haiti at the end of his life. Not only did it set a new example for the need to merge the arts, such as writing and painting, but, by comparing the paintings of Saint-Soleil with the frescoes by James Ensor, Malraux continued the revolution begun by cannibalism and Surrealism to enrich human perception and make room for artistic creations from Elsewhere just as Picasso's *Demoiselles d'Avignon* thrust Art Nègre (or Art by Negroes) into the spotlight of Western Art.

Yet in my eyes the artist who incarnates best the artistic plurality generated by the *Lands of the Atlantic* is Romare Bearden.

7 André Breton, *Manifestoes of Surrealism* (Richard Seaver and Helen R. Lane trans) (Ann Arbor: University of Michigan Press, 1969), p. 14.

Unlike the previous voyages, Bearden's ancestors were transplanted from Africa and he was born in the South of the USA. Like the first couple of Oswald and Tarsila, Bearden and his wife are an example of artistic companionship. Nanette Rohan-Bearden was a dancer and choreographer. Bearden was to spend the last seventeen years of his life with her on the island of Saint-Martin and often visited Martinique, the 'snake charmer', which exerted on him its legendary fascination. In my opinion, Bearden was a model. From 1964 onward, he made collages which brought him international attention, thus proving that there is no minor artistic expression. He was the embodiment of the ideal union of artistic creations. For his wife's dance company, he handled fabrics and materials and created scenery as well as costumes. He was also a musician, a great connoisseur of jazz and the blues, and a friend of Duke Ellington. For many years he gave up painting for music and founded the Bluebird Music Company which was a great success with audiences. One revealing detail was the fact that he often compared his paintings to musical improvisations and claimed they were the visual equivalents of the blues.[8] Bearden, furthermore, symbolized the collapse of the barriers between the Races and Cultures and devoted part of his work to translating with his brush the poetry of the Spaniard Federico García Lorca.

The question now is: What is the legacy of these voyages, these encounters and these exchanges? What footprints have they left? Do the artists of *Lands of the Atlantic* know that they already hold the answer to many of these questions?

8 See Richard and Sally Price, *Romare Bearden: The Caribbean Dimension* (Philadelphia: University of Pennsylvania Press, 2006).

The cultural action at stake today has changed in nature. The battle for 'difference' or 'authenticity', once two key notions, seems to be lost; perhaps too the notion of cultural identity, at least in its monolithic meaning. Identity can only be plural since the world has no longer fixed frontiers or borders. In the global village thus named by Marshall McLuhan in 1968, everything merges and cultural hierarchies are eliminated. Forty years ago, Martinican Frantz Fanon could denounce a partitioned world, divided in two: the colonial world and the colonized world. More recently, Trinidadian V. S. Naipaul lamented that, in order to create, the individual had to be transplanted (wishful thinking, he said) from the periphery to the centre, i.e. from the world of nature to that with a tradition of culture:

> The writing of books, the publishing of books, may be taken for granted by people who belong to a society in which those activities are part of the social routine. [. . .] But I don't spring out of that kind of society, and that is why I have felt that I am floating in a vacuum. I am an oddity, and have always felt that I was an oddity, since I have always been writing . . .[9]

Such affirmations and lamentations are no longer valid today. What does the word 'colonies' cover? If we keep to its primary meaning of dependent territory, the world is full of colonies, even though the trappings of domination have disappeared. On the other hand, Naipaul's wishful

9 Bharati Mukherjee and Robert Boyers, 'A Conversation with V. S. Naipaul' (1981) in Feroza F. Jussawalla (ed.), *Conversations with V. S. Naipaul* (Jackson: University Press of Mississippi, 1997), pp. 75–92; here, pp. 75–6.

thinking has come about. In our century of migration and transfer of people, many from the peripheral regions have been forced to settle in Europe, Canada and the USA where they practise their art. Just as they have changed their place of residence so they have changed languages. The world's underlying bastions of binary oppositions have collapsed, overcome by the hegemony of economic power.

In 1989, Martinican poet Monchoachi asks:

Where is the Caribbean? Where is its location?
Where is the soil, where is the site, where is the place?[10]

And we could add: Where is the Centre? Where is the Periphery? Do such notions still exist? Moping for the Orient, all Flaubert need do is to make the rounds of certain Paris neighbourhoods.

Lands of the Atlantic anticipates these developments, so liberating in more than one respect that we could easily mistake them for being confusing. These lands have long been a melting pot from where the elements of what we call today 'world culture' have spread. This culture with no exact origin, no borders, steeped in multiple influences, is constantly in movement and resists definition.

'The earth is not round, not yet, we have to make it round,' said Henri Michaux.[11]

Was he thinking of these lands of the Atlantic whose artists are on display today?

Surely not.

10 Monchoachi, *La case où se tient la lune*, pp. 7–10.

11 Henri Michaux, *Ecuador* (Paris: Gallimard, 1929), p. 82.

Sketching a Literature from the French Antilles

FROM NEGRITUDE TO CRÉOLITÉ

When the islanders of Guadeloupe and Martinique get together they tell a story of how one day the Good Lord woke up feeling bored. The earth seemed so empty with its flamboyants, its mapou trees and the sea that never wearied of lashing out at the rocks. Something was missing, something that would add a little imagination, create a little chaos. That's how God got the idea of creating Man. He gathered up a little sand from the seashore, kneaded it, rolled it, and made His first figure which He then put in an oven to bake. Then He went and lay beneath a tree and fell asleep. The smell of something burning woke Him up. It was His first version of Man that had come out all burnt and black, no use to anyone. He threw it away as far as He could and set to work again, harder than ever. But the same thing happened again. He fell asleep while His creature was in the oven, and when He awoke with a start he found

Inaugural Lecture at the Maison Francaise, Buell Hall, Columbia University on 29 November 1995. First published in *Black Renaissance/ Renaissance Noire* 1(1) (Fall 1996): 138–63. [Bloomington: Indiana University Press]. Also available in: Timothy J. Reiss (ed.), *Sisyphus and Eldorado: Magical and Other Realisms in Caribbean Literature*, 2nd rev. edn (Trenton, NJ: Africa World Press, 2002), pp. 211–24.

it a little over-baked, slightly too brown. Once more He went to work, this time determined to demonstrate His talents as Creator. His third version turned out perfect, the colour of the waxing moon. He hugged it to his heart out of sheer joy.

The first creature that had come out black, ugly and useless, was the ancestor of the black man; the second the mulatto; while the third, the one He clasped to his heart, the one He preferred in its perfection, was the forefather of the white man.

Though it may be a folktale, this story has all the makings of a myth of origin, for isn't a myth of origin nothing less than how a people sees itself symbolically within the world and its relationship with the rest of the universe? I would say that, to a certain extent, the entire history of the literature of the Lesser Antilles is composed of the ceaseless efforts of its writers to uproot this myth from the collective unconscious, this seemingly innocent tale of creation that is nonetheless loaded with negative values, and to replace it with another, more befitting the pain and complexity of the islands' history or, as Césaire put it, 'to grow a tree of sulfur and lava amidst a defeated people.'[1]

The Caribbean region is like a stage on which actors in an assortment of costumes, speaking different tongues and consequently incapable of communicating, enter, exit, cross paths, come face to face and often clash, uttering discourses intelligible to their ears alone. The first to enter the stage are the Spaniards, headed by Columbus. He bears the rank of admiral, originally the more familiar Arabic term, emir or commander, adopted into the Spanish by Alfonso X. Columbus is surrounded by his men, one of whom is the

---

1 Césaire, *And the Dogs Were Silent* in *Lyric and Dramatic Poetry*, p. 43.

writer of the fleet, Rodrigo Descobedo, who has recorded the position of the new lands. The Spaniards wear helmets, full suits of armour and leather boots. Columbus holds between his hands the standard of Ferdinand of Aragon and Isabella of Spain which bears a cross, two crowns and the letters *F* and *Y* intertwined on a background of dark red velvet. Facing him, assembled on the shore, are the Indians, quite naked: 'They have no iron, nor steel, nor weapons, nor are they fit for them, because although they are well-made men of commanding stature, they appear extraordinarily timid.'[2] Of course the Indians do not understand Spanish. They understand nothing therefore of the brief interlude played out in front of them. They are oblivious to the fact that they have just been dispossessed of their lands where their fathers and forefathers were born and which have just been named San Salvador, Santa Maria de Concepcion, Fernandina, Isabella and Isla Juana.

I emphasize the difference in attire between the Spaniards and the Indians, the former clothed from head to toe, the latter stark naked, because this external contrast symbolizes the opposition that was henceforth to dominate Europe's colonial discourse. Civilization versus barbarity, the clothed versus the unclothed, or people who write versus people who don't, whose language remains unrevealed by the Christian God and therefore excluded from the *logos*. The Spaniards and other European nationalities who were to fight for the possession of the Caribbean islands never held an equivocal discourse on the Indians. Who were they?

2 Christopher Columbus, 'The Letter of Columbus to Luis de Sant Angel Announcing His Discovery' (1493) in Charles W. Eliot (ed.), *American Historical Documents, 1000–1904*, VOL. 43 (New York: P. F. Collier & Son, 1909–14), pp. 22–8; here, p. 24.

Were they the paradisiacal ancestors of the human race or were they savages, cannibals that the Europeans had every right to subjugate? In 1537, Pope Paul III's ironically titled *Sublimis Deus* would finally concede the Indians' humanity. Yet we might very well ask ourselves whether the subsequent dichotomy that would emerge in colonial anthropology between the Caribs and the Arawaks does not date back to this divided perception. Cannibals or not, the Indians would exit the Caribbean stage, decimated by disease, mistreatment and hard labour. They would leave behind them the scent of annatto, mysterious drawings engraved on the rocks and a few words that would become part of the language of the islands—*ajoupa, carbet, boucan*—only to reappear a few centuries later in the mythical memory of writers as Caliban, the character borrowed from Shakespeare, to exhort the islanders to take up the struggle again.

In the footsteps of the Indians come the massive numbers of 'Those who have invented neither gunpowder nor the compass [. . .] those who have explored neither the seas nor the sky',[3] in other words, the Africans snatched from the ports of Africa—naked as well. Never would they have the words of a Bartolome de las Casas to defend them, and the place reserved for them would be the last rungs of the ladder of humanity. What I find remarkable is that this 'vomit of a slave-ship', as Césaire calls them in his *Notebook*, came to stay.[4] Despite the pain of exile in these Caribbean lands, the harsh treatment and the rigours of slavery, the Africans would grow and multiply like the grass from that Guinea (Nan-Djinin) they would keep in their memory. They would invent the Creole language which would enable

3 Césaire, *Notebook*, p. 111.

4 Ibid., p. 107.

them to communicate among themselves and convey both the knowledge they inherited from Africa as well as the one forged in their new environment. They would invent a music with the instruments from the lost continent—the drum, the *tambour ka*, the flute, the *ti bwa*—and with those borrowed from their new masters from Europe. They would snatch secrets from the plants, the wind, the rivers and the sea. After them, other actors were to emerge on the already crowded Caribbean stage—the Indians from South India embarked from the trading posts of Pondicherry and Karikal and those from the provinces of Bihar, Bengal and Orissa who boarded ship in Calcutta.

For almost four centuries, the voices of these actors would never be heard. One voice of authority would dominate and one alone, the guardians of colonial power, the Europeans from all walks of life: planters, missionaries and travellers. The first would complain of the vices of the Negroes and mulattoes; the latter would deplore the lack of any cultural life, the diabolical thirst for lucre of the white Creoles and the lasciviousness of their women. Now and then the traveller would pen a few sorrowful lines on the slaves' condition. But, generally speaking, the vision of the European visitor is aligned with that of the masters. Both think that the Negroes, reject of nature, are machines whose springs need rewinding. Until finally the Caribbean voice splutters, then explodes.

'What do you expect,' asked Sartre 'when you remove the gag from these black mouths? That they will start singing your praises? Here are black men standing tall, looking us straight in the eyes, and I hope you feel as I do, the sudden emotion of being revealed.'[5]

5 Sartre, 'Black Orpheus' in *The Aftermath of War*, p. 259 (translation modified).

In what follows I shall limit myself to the French-speaking Lesser Antilles, the islands of Guadeloupe and Martinique, focusing on their writers, situated at different periods in the cultural development of the islands: Saint-John Perse, Aimé Césaire and Simone Schwarz-Bart. Why these in particular? First, for purely subjective reasons. And because their comparison, I believe, symbolizes the contrast, the contradictions, the dissonance and the infinite diversity of our island literature which we should be careful not to reduce to a single school.

Except for poetry, Saint-John Perse and Aimé Césaire are worlds apart. The former, a white Creole of planter stock, a *béké*, as we say in the islands, born on an islet anchored off Guadeloupe. The latter, the black son of a plantation bursar and seamstress, born in a sugar-growing area of Martinique. Perse, a 'precocious Creole' with the makings of a fine consul, in the opinion of Paul Claudel, a career diplomat who, even in his setbacks and exile in the USA, would never lose his powerful friends. Césaire, mayor of Fort-de-France, beloved by the common folk as Papa Aimé. The former would accumulate awards, the Grand Prix National des Lettres, the Grand Prix International de Poésie, the Nobel Prize for Literature, the highest recompense for a writer, and finally, acceptance into the prestigious Pléiade Collection during his lifetime. The latter, considered the founding father of black literature, nevertheless finds himself in his old age under violent, often unjust, attacks from a young generation of writers, 'the demolition team'.[6]

6 See Annie Le Brun, *Pour Aimé Césaire* (Paris: Jean-Michel Place, 1994).

Even more striking, their conception of the role of the writer is markedly different. Perse declares while denouncing, even denying, his Guadeloupean origins: 'Any localization or dating seems loathsome to me for our paltry entertainments of the mind.'[7] Césaire writes: 'I come to this land of mine and I would say: "Kiss me without fear . . . And if I can only speak, it is for you that I shall speak." '[8]

Simone Schwarz-Bart, my third writer, is a woman. She is the descendant of an already long tradition of women writers but she is the first to have escaped marginalization and to have mingled her score with the concert of men. Even Suzanne Césaire, despite her decisive contribution to the magazine *Tropiques*, remains in our memories as merely the 'glow of rum punch' that gleamed in the eyes of André Breton during his stay in Martinique.[9]

Perse was for a long time a problematic figure in Antillean literature. Initially, the vision of the world by this white planter's son, who seemed oblivious to his conscience and made no critical judgement on the colonial capitalist order, exasperated and shocked the majority of the islanders, who were little concerned with the literary

7 Saint-John Perse, 'Letter to Valery Darbaud, December 1911', in *Œuvres complètes* (Paris: Bibliothèque de la Pléiade, Gallimard, 1972), p. 793.

8 Césaire, *Notebook*, p. 87.

9 André Breton, 'Un grand poète noir' (1943), preface to *Cahier d'un retour au pays natal/Memorandum on My Martinique*, bilingual edn (Lionel Abel and Yvann Goll trans) (New York: Brentano's, 1947), unpaginated. Another translation of this preface—'The Great Black Poet' (Annette Smith and Clayton Eshleman trans)—is available at: webdelsol.com/Sulfur/Breton_text.htm (last accessed 14 August 2013).

qualities of his work. Perse made no mystery of the fact; the world he eulogizes in *Éloges*, the world of his childhood paradise, is the world of the plutocracy, of demigods perched at the top of the social pyramid. No indignation here with the colonial hierarchy, unlike Jean-Marie Le Clézio, another white Creole. In 'Ecrit sur la porte', the opening lines of *Éloges*, Perse writes with total disregard for his fellow islanders of another race:

> My pride is that my daughter should be very beautiful when she gives orders to the black women,
> my joy, that she should have a very white arm among her black hens.[10]

With the same insensitivity, he states in 'To Celebrate a Childhood':

> [A]nd I never knew all the women and all the men who served in our high
> wooden house; but I shall still long remember mute faces, the colour of papaya and of boredom, that paused like burnt-out stars behind our chairs.[11]

For Perse, despite the abolition of slavery and the ensuing social upheavals, the Negro, the mulatto and the Indian remain but servants, hardly moving objects, useful but with no visible singularity. Through the poems in *Éloges*, the planters' society and the order of the plantation economy are set in place. Dress, behaviour and lifestyle— all converge to define the poet socially. The adjectives

10 Saint-John Perse, 'Written on the Door' in *Éloges and Other Poems*, p. 3.

11 Saint-John Perse, 'To Celebrate a Childhood' in *Éloges and Other Poems*, p. 17.

'white' and 'high' are obsessively repeated. Yet, as we turn the pages, this blight fades away and we are left with the smell, the shape and the light of the vegetation and the island: 'I awake dreaming of the black fruit of the Aniba; of flowers in bundles under the axil of the leaves.'[12]

What we see is the commotion in the streets of Pointe-à-Pitre, the scenes of everyday life. Especially in the first version of *Éloges*, there are many examples designating local realities and even words of Creole speech, such as *mornes*, *cayes*, *sirop batterie*, *boucaut*, *l'herbe de Man Lalie*, *icaquiers*, *anolis* and the *annao* bird straight out of a Creole lullaby. And gradually we realize that this voice is a necessary factor for it expresses one side of our history. Derek Walcott understood this full well when he stated: 'We cannot deny him any more than we can Aimé Césaire.'[13]

Martinican writer Glissant goes further, so much so that he ends up in a fraternal identification with Perse whom he considers his white double. In his poem 'Les Indes' (1956), Glissant takes up the rhythms and themes of Perse to describe the other side of the conquistador epic, the red side, or the extermination of the Indians—and the black side, or the slave trade, concluding: 'Thus Perse was often in the clearing of my words.'[14]

12 Saint-John Perse, 'Praises' in *Éloges and Other Poems*, p. 28.

13 Derek Walcott, 'The Antilles: Fragments of Epic Memory', Nobel Lecture, 7 December 1992. Available at: www.nobelprize.org/nobel_prizes/literature/laureates/1992/walcott-lecture.html (last accessed 14 August 2013).

14 See Édouard Glissant, *The Indies*, bilingual edn (Dominique O'Neill trans.) (Toronto: Éditions du Gref, 1992). The line about Perse may be located in Édouard Glissant, 'Saint-John Perse et les Antillais', *Nouvelle Revue Française. Hommage à Saint-John Perse* 278 (February 1976): 68–74, here, p. 73.

Another person who saw the complementarity between Perse and Césaire was André Breton, who united both poets in a common admiration. 'Saint-John Perse,' he wrote in the first Surrealist Manifesto, 'is Surrealist at a distance.'[15]

Little is known of the frequent visits Breton paid to the poet-diplomat while Perse was working at the Foreign Ministry, Quai d'Orsay, and we are eagerly awaiting publication of a correspondence that will shed more light on this matter.[16]

I personally would like to compare Columbus with Breton landing on Martinique in April 1941. Of course, the differences between the two men are enormous. Columbus was dispatched by a country. Breton was fleeing his country, which had once again been dragged reluctantly into war. But both had the power to discover, to name and rename. As he did with Perse, Breton baptized Césaire with the name Surrealist.

The story that follows is almost a household legend. During his stopover in Martinique, Breton went shopping for a ribbon for his daughter. In a haberdasher's shop he came across a copy of the magazine *Tropiques* published by Aimé and Suzanne Césaire and a group of loyal friends that included René Ménil and Jules Monnerot. In the words of critic Régis Antoine, the encounter took on a mythical nature since the 'marvellous ribbon' for his daughter led him straight to René Ménil, and then to Aimé Césaire whom he was surprised to discover 'to be of such a pure

---

15 Breton, *Manifestoes of Surrealism*, p. 27.

16 See *Europe*, 799–800 (Special Issue on Saint-John Perse, Henriette Levillain and Mireille Sacotte eds) (November–December 1995): 59–84.

black, all the more masked at first sight because he was smiling.'[17] Breton would later write a preface to a new edition of *Notebook of a Return to My Native Land* that had been published completely unnoticed a few years earlier, and conclude with this surrealist image: 'The speech of Aimé Césaire, as heady as nascent oxygen.'[18]

Breton has been subsequently criticized for having contemplated Césaire and Martinique, the inspiration for his text *Martinique, charmeuse de serpents* (1948), as a dreamer who meets a portion of his dream at a bend in the river.[19] Yet Césaire himself has never countered this appropriation and baptism by Breton. At the most, during an interview with critic Jacqueline Leiner, he stated: 'When Breton read the first three issues of *Tropiques*, he believed I was a Surrealist. This was not entirely true, yet it was not entirely false. The meeting with Breton confirmed what I had discovered on my own.'[20]

What had he discovered on his own? That the poet must not let himself be downcast by the divorce between action and dreams? That a poem must be a debacle of the intellect? That if beauty is not convulsive it is nothing? That a stunning image is not born out of a comparison but by closing the gap between two remote realities?

17 Régis Antoine, *La littérature franco-antillaise* (Paris: Karthala, 1992), p. 264. For Breton's account of this episode, see n9.

18 Breton, 'Un grand poète noir'.

19 André Breton, *Martinique, charmeuse de serpents* (Paris: Jean-Jacques Pauvert, 1972). Availalble in English as: *Martinique, Snake Charmer* (David W. Seaman trans., Franklin Rosemont introd., with drawings and texts by André Masson) (Austin: University of Texas Press, 2008).

20 See Jacqueline Leiner, 'Entretien avec A.C.' in Aime Césaire (ed.), *Tropiques* 1 (Paris: Jean-Michel Place, 1978), pp. 29–33.

The work of Césaire is a unique phenomenon for it manages to reconcile factors that seem irreconcilable— Negritude, i.e. the entrenchment in race, and universalism; Surrealism and the commitment to a political ideology, and even, to a certain extent, socialist realism.

Just as the very substance of Perse's work is the planter plutocracy and the white Creoles, so Césaire's is 'the nigger scum, the nigger scum reeking of fried onions' that Césaire wants to stand tall and free. The theses of his Negritude are initially simple and clear-cut, almost simplistic, we are tempted to say today. He refutes the notion of ethnic and cultural *métissage* that his friend Senghor was already defending. According to Césaire, whether the Caribbean man is light or dark-skinned, he is a black man. Alienated by slavery and colonization, he has disowned his origins. It is important for him, therefore, to return to the source of his culture and his race, i.e. Africa, not in order to cut himself off from the rest of humanity but to make a con-tribution specific to the Black World.

'To write,' says Maurice Blanchot, 'is to pass from the first to the third person, so that what happens to me hap-pens to no one.'[21] Not for Césaire. To write is to switch from 'I' to 'us' so that what happens to everyone else hap-pens to him as well. In a Pan-Negro expansionism, he claims as his the heritage of the African American and the Haitian before becoming 'a Jew-man, a kaffir-man, a Hindu-from-Calcutta-man',[22] i.e. before embracing all of humanity in its suffering.

---

21 Maurice Blanchot, 'The Essential Solitude' (1955) in *The Space of Literature* (Ann Smock trans. and introd.) (Lincoln: University of Nebraska Press, 1982), p. 33.

22 Césaire, *Notebook*, p. 85.

A close analysis of *Tropiques* reveals this attempt to break away from the particular, despite the isolation caused by the war. Not only did the magazine shatter Suzanne Césaire's exotic triad, 'hibiscus, frangipani, bougainvillea',[23] in order to re-establish the colonized subject in his 'pahouin ugliness';[24] not only did it explore the confines of Martinican identity but it also endeavoured to build up contacts with its neighbours of the New World and, thirty years before *Antillanité*, to place Martinique in a radically new relationship. On a personal level, neighbourly contacts were being established. It was during this period that Césaire became friends with Cubans Lydia Cabrera, Wifredo Lam (who was to illustrate his work) and Alejo Carpentier. Negritude is not a narrowly territorialized discourse of a limiting nature but an attempt at open-mindedness. Now that the ideology of Pan-Africanism is practically moribund and the notion of culture is replacing race, Negritude is criticized for taking the black race as its only foundation. For what harnesses human to human in countries like the islands of the Caribbean, composed of hybrids and half-castes, is not colour or forefather but culture. Negritude is criticized therefore for having been unable to find words that tie the descendant of the white man to that of the black and the East Indian or all three. Perhaps the historical context of its birth has not been sufficiently taken into account.

One might very well think that Césaire's endeavour at self-rediscovery would make use of all the facets of the islands' resources and would sooner or later come up

23 See Suzanne Césaire, 'Misère d'une poésie: John Antoine-Nau', *Tropiques* 4 (January 1942): 48–50.

24 Césaire, *Notebook*, p. 97.

against the problem of language and the coexistence of French and Creole in the French Antilles. A number of Martinican and Guadeloupean linguists have studied the diglossia of the French Antilles. According to conventional binary opposition, French is the language of colonization and Creole the mother tongue or, in the words of Paul Ricoeur, the language that expresses a surplus of meaning.[25] Césaire is undoubtedly sensitive to the contradiction that consists of uttering the shout of the black soul in the language imposed by the white master and of 'this anguish like none other / From taming with the words from France / This heart that came to me from Senegal.'[26] In his own way, he attempts to subvert the French language by inventing neologisms, scholarly words with a Greek or Latin root.

Obviously, the burning question is whether the insertion of the Creole language in a work makes it more *authentic*. However, the facts are there. Unlike Perse, the white Creole, whose layer of Creole lexis has been highlighted by the Martinican Emile Yoyo, Césaire's language remains virtually untouched by the tongue born in the universe of the plantation. In the interview with Leiner, in answer to why *Tropiques* was not written in Creole, he retorts that such a question is meaningless—because such a journal would be inconceivable in Creole. And, by way of elaboration, he adds that one of the causes of Martinique's cultural backwardness is the register of language, of Créolité that has

25 See Paul Ricoeur, *Interpretation Theory: Discourse and the Surplus of Meaning* (Fort Worth: Texas Christian University Press, 1976).

26 Léon Laleau, 'Trahison' (1931) in Senghor, *Anthologie*, p. 108. Available in English as 'Betrayal' (Ellen Conroy Kennedy trans.) in Stewart Brown and Mark McWatt (eds), *The Oxford Book of Caribbean Verse* (New York: Oxford University Press, 2009), p. 9.

remained at the stage of immediacy, incapable either of elevation or the expression of abstract ideas.

Yet, very early on, the Creole tongue, spoken by slaves and masters alike, attracted the attention of Europeans living in the islands. Generally speaking, it is looked upon as a dialect, a patois, a pidgin French, reserved, as Césaire has mentioned, for expressing the immediate. It is not written. Consequently, it has neither grammar nor spelling and is shunned by schools and the administration. Yet everyone appreciates what they call its picturesque and colourful nature. In the early eighteenth century, François-Achille Marbot, a settler from Martinique, transcribed into Creole the fables of La Fontaine (1817–66).[27] In the nineteenth century, Greek traveller Lafcadio Hearn, like André Breton, fell in love with Martinique. Unlike Breton, he was not carried away by the work of a poet but by the women of the common folk, the washerwomen, the women who dyed the madras head ties, the market women with trays on their heads whose dialogues he transcribed in *Youma*: *The Story of a West Indian Slave* (1890) and *Trois fois bel conte* (1939): 'Bonjou, Mayotte! Bonjou Chèchelle! Kouman ou kale Rina ma chè?' ('Good day, Mayotte! Good day, Chéchelle! How are you, my dear Rina?)[28]

27 François-Achille Marbot, *Les Bambous, fables de La Fontaine, travesties en patois créole, par un vieux commandeur* (Fort-de-France, Martinique: Libraire de Frédéric Thomas, 1869). Available at: gallica.bnf.fr/ ark:/12148/bpt6k 54261407 (last accessed 14 August 2013).

28 Lafcadio Hearn, *Youma: The Story of a West Indian Slave* (New York: Harper and Brothers, 1890). Available at: library.uoregon.edu/ec/e-asia/read/youma.pdf (last accessed 14 August 2013); *Trois fois bel conte* (Serge Denis trans.) (Paris: Mercure de France, 1939). Available at: classiques.uqac.ca/classiques/hearn_lafcadio/trois_fois_bel_conte/ trois_ fois_ bel_conte.html (last accessed 14 August 2013).

It goes without saying this is an exotic, folksy adulteration. For the islanders themselves, the Creole orature very soon emerges as the refuge of a counter-culture—the plantation culture versus assimilation. It appears to verbalize a cultural resistance. Brandishing it therefore appears as a prelude to any revolution. As early as 1935, the claim to cultural independence—failing any other—that was so clear to Césaire merged in the minds of certain intellectuals with that of linguistic independence. Martinican poet Gilbert Gratiant, a member of the Communist party, wrote *Cinq Poèmes Martiniquais* (1936) which he combined with a literary and artistic programme and in which he stated: 'Creole? I want to codify its writing, establish a grammar and hold a conference with all the Creole scholars of the Caribbean region . . . I want to forge weapons of deliverance out of what I have acquired from the white civilization with what I have safeguarded from the black through the Creole language.'[29]

Fab'Compè Zicaq (1948, The Fables of Brother Zicaq), which he subsequently published, still in Creole, is worthy of attention.[30] It is an inventory of the spirit, the philosophy, the humour, alienation and richness of the Creole mentality. But we cannot help noting that they would never be the cultural weapons of deliverance he dreamt of. These would be rather the texts by Césaire written in French. Nevertheless, the reproach, that Césaire did not take into sufficient consideration the colonial dimension of the French language, is not without justification.

29 Gilbert Gratiant, *Cinq Poèmes Martiniquais* (Hauteville, Ain: n.p., 1936).

30 Gilbert Gratiant, *Fab'Compè Zicaq* (Fort-de-France: Désormeaux, 1948).

Unless . . . unless Césaire the surrealist realized that for the writer and the poet all languages are foreign, that there is no mother tongue. It is by dynamiting the forest of established signs, markers and beacons that the poet blazes his trail. In *Caribbean Discourse*, Glissant denounces the mad streak in our people's meaningless speech and, afraid that Creole culture is being reduced to nothingness, proposes an archaeology of the Maroon tongue so that the buried voice of the people can be heard. Bernabé, Chamoiseau and Confiant caution: 'Every time a mother, thinking she is favoring the learning of the French language, represses Creole in a child's throat, is in fact bearing a blow to the latter's imagination, repressing his creativity.'[31]

But it was the novelist Simone Schwarz-Bart who was the first to have attempted a radically different reading of Caribbean reality in a literary text written in French. Much has been said about the feminine—I did not say *feminist*—revolution brought about by Schwarz-Bart. It is a fact. In a literary field saturated with messianic heroes, be they poetic or proletarian, *The Bridge of Beyond* ([1972] 1974) plunges us into a fabulous story of women, the chronicle of the Lougandors, a mythical line of matrons.[32] Yet something would be lacking if we saw it merely as, for example, *Masters of the Dew* ([1944] 1947), where a family of women are playing their version of Manuel.[33] In comparison with

31 Bernabé, Chamoiseau and Confiant, 'In Praise of Creoleness', p. 899.

32 Simone Schwarz-Bart, *The Bridge of Beyond* (Barbara Bray trans., Jamaica Kincaid introd.) (New York: New York Review of Books, 2013).

33 Jacques Roumain, *Masters of the Dew: A Novel of Haiti* (Mercer Cook and Langston Hughes trans, J. Michael Dash introd.) (New York: Heinemann, 1978).

these pre-texts, Schwarz-Bart innovates. She innovated by *metamorphosing* the Creole oral tradition. In one of her rare interviews, she reveals the finality of her work when she says that a language is, above all, communication. If bits of Creole artifices have to be inserted into the French, then it means one has failed. Above all, she says, she had wanted to convey the spirit of the Creole language.[34]

The spirit of the Creole language! We would like to learn more, for these words are important. Unfortunately, that's all she says. If we study the text, we find no glossary. No collages or idiomatic lexical inlays. No neologisms. A few irregular constructions modelled on the Creole. In short, there is no deliberate effort to transcribe or even translate literally from Creole. And yet the absent corpus of the Creole language cries out to us. Linguists are still puzzling over the nature of the process used in such a superficially transparent text: Is it a shift in semantics, masterfully controlled archaisms or, in according to Bernabé, embroidered proverbs?

Between Two Worlds ([1979] 1981), the second text by Schwarz-Bart, not as popular as the first because it is more disconcerting, poses further questions. The language is more French, with hints of archaisms here and there. Consequently, its *Créolité* lies elsewhere. We begin to have some clue if we compare *Between Two Worlds* with *Macunaíma* by Brazilian writer Mário de Andrade. Like *Macunaíma*, a fairytale character is transplanted into the universe of the novel, i.e. there is a shift from the collective to the individual. But

34 Hélène and Roger Toumson, 'Interview avec Simone et André Schwarz-Bart: Sur les pas de Fanotte' (1979) in *Textes et Etudes Documents*, 2 (*Pluie et vent sur Télumée Miracle de Simone Schwarz-Bart*) (1979): 13–23.

unlike the Brazilian text, *Between Two Worlds* is not written as a baroque compilation of oral knowledge (myths, legends, pharmacopoeia) but as a picturesque variation on an oral tradition that serves as a support for a personal reflection. Ti-Jean disengages himself from the canon of orature and becomes a modern hero committed to a personal search for the Caribbean identity. In his own way, Ti-Jean turns his back on Africa and thus refutes Negritude. He also turns his back on Europe and paves the way for a syncretic Caribbean identity that does not reserve pride of place for the Creole language alone.

In short, Schwarz-Bart seems to be saying that the desire to transplant Creole orature into writing or to claim to be the guardian of the Creole tongue when one is a writer is an appealing but impossible ambition. Writing is the death knell of orature. The task of communicating—and possibly enchanting—must be pursued in other ways. The telling must be relayed in another fashion. She is short on explanations and rejects the militancy and theorizing of the chattering intellectuals because she would surely agree with Nathalie Sarraute's words: '[A] great novel is like St Petersburg built on marshlands, like Venice wrested, at the cost of what effort, from the turgid waters of the lagoons.'[35]

No one wants to hear of the drainage works in the lagoon. What matters are the palaces on the Grand Canal. Likewise, each writer must forge his own canon in silence as best he can, because any stroke of inspiration that lays down the law very soon runs the risk of becoming a strategy and a system.

35 Nathalie Sarraute, *The Golden Fruits* (Maria Jolas trans.) (New York: George Braziller, 1964), p. 39.

Many have criticized these novels, especially *The Bridge of Beyond*, for their fatalist vision of the Caribbean reality. There is no denunciation of oppression and colonial exploitation, they lament. There is no revolutionary message or blueprint. Caroline Oudin-Bastide, in the now defunct journal *CARE*, makes the harsh, unenlightened judgement that by privileging characters controlled by destiny, yet conscious of their dignity and their respectability, Schwarz-Bart places herself far below the level of alienation criticized by the Negritude writers.[36]

The reason for such judgements is that the notion of commitment and socialist realism loom like the shadow of the Statue of the Commander over Caribbean literature. Many, in calling for positive heroes and exemplary tales, still confuse literature and political tract. They would like the writer's voice to speak of the misfortunes of the voiceless and hark back to the days when poetical ambition merged with political ambition. Many are those who still speak of the role and mission of the writer in the task of building up their people's awareness. Though some have gone so far as to scorn 'the black protests and other libertarian bugbears so poorly formulated by the epigones of Negritude',[37] the writers of the French Antilles in general have become more cautious. They are fully aware that Césaire's *Discourse on Colonialism* was written in 1955 and that today their islands are still not only colonies of France but also colonies of Europe. They know they are familiar figures on the islands but seldom read and, consequently, prevented from exerting any influence whatsoever through

---

36 Caroline Oudin-Bastide, '*Pluie et Vent sur Télumée Miracle*: fatalisme et aliénation', *CARE*, 2 (1974): 83–97.

37 Chamoiseau and Confiant, *Lettres creoles*, p. 184.

their writings. All too often their impact is measured by the number of articles, and especially TV programmes, devoted to them. But they know too that the punch of the picture is not the same as the power of the pen. All this has led them to challenge the sacrosanct notion of commitment they inherited from Sartre and perhaps the collective cultural concept of the Negro-African world prior to him.

What is commitment in literature? A literature that accuses, or quite simply one that lifts the veil and is food for thought and dreams? And what if, as Alain Robbe-Grillet believes, the only realm over which a writer can reign is that of his language?[38] Since the Caribbean writer no longer lives in the great white mirage and no longer models his writing on European lines, doesn't a work that manages to subvert the form of the Western novel in its narrative strategy and structure also deserve to be called revolutionary—perhaps more so than any other? Isn't the fundamental issue to make a specific contribution to the world of literature?

All these questions are still being hotly debated.

I feel a great regret at not having mentioned Haiti, for despite all its tribulations and upheavals Haiti is ever present in the hearts and minds of the writers from Martinique and Guadeloupe. It is worth pausing to study how Haiti has been represented in the imagination of our writers. They first appropriated the gallery of historical, legendary generals—the 'brocaded Africans' as Napoleon called them: Toussaint Louverture, the conqueror turned martyr, 'an old wog rising against the waters of the sky' (Césaire);[39]

38 See Alain Robbe-Grillet, *For a New Novel* (Evanston, IL: Northwestern University Press, 1992).

39 Césaire, *Notebook*, p. 91.

Dessalines and his awesome shout *Coupé têt, brilé kaye* (cut off heads and burn the houses); and Christophe who killed himself with a golden bullet in his palace of Sans Souci. The major writers of the French Antilles—Aimé Césaire, Édouard Glissant and Vincent Placoly—were to appropriate these eponymous heroes into their theatre and to enrich their writings with ideas from Haitian intellectuals. Negritude's place of birth was not just Paris and the Left Bank but first of all Port-au-Prince and perhaps Léogane as well, where the rebel Charlemagne Péralte was crucified.

Suddenly, with the end of the Duvalier years, everything changes. The stuff of myths crumbles. The Haitian refugees invade everyone's conscience. The tragedy of the boat people replaces the tragedy of King Christophe, and the distress of today's Haiti thrusts itself on our imagination. In her play *Your Handsome Captain* ([1987] 1989), Schwarz-Bart is worlds away from the excesses of a half-crazed emperor.[40] It is the humble story of an outcast, a Haitian exiled on the island of Guadeloupe, his only ties with his lost land being a set of cassettes, the epistles of modern correspondence, where the voice of his beloved wife provides a presence out of absence.

An important voice in the *diversalité* (cleverly coined by Confiant and Chamoiseau) of Haitian works, the writer Frankétienne contributes a genuine tour de force. In *Dézafi* (1975) and *Les affres d'un défi* (1979), he presents two versions of the same story, one in Creole, the other in French.[41] I say 'two versions' for one text is neither the

---

40 Simone Schwarz-Bart, *Your Handsome Captain* (Jessica Harris and Catherine Temerson trans), *Callaloo* 40 (Summer 1989): 531–43.

41 Frankétienne, *Dézafi* (Port-au-Prince: Fardin, 1975); *Les affres d'un défi* (Port-au-Prince: Deschamps, 1979).

translation of the other nor its transposition. Frankétienne demonstrates that the imagination, the language and the narrative structure of a novel in Creole are distinct from those in French.

Lastly, Haitian literature poses a number of issues that sooner or later the literature from Guadeloupe and Martinique will have to confront, if this is not already the case. Who is the Haitian, Martinican and Guadeloupean writer? An individual fortunate enough to live on the island? Is someone forced into exile still a Caribbean writer? Can the Créolité of Haiti, Guadeloupe and Martinique survive uprooting? Can it speak other languages apart from the original French and Creole? Can it speak English?

As I have too quickly endeavoured to show, the paths of French Caribbean literature are tortuous. After Césaire's Negritude, Glissant's Antillanité is wary of falling into any illusion, be it European or African. According to Glissant, the Caribbean region has the vocation to be the richest, the most extraordinary and the most open-minded of syntheses, i.e. the propensity to relate. Much attention has been paid to the writers of Créolité, namely Confiant and Chamoiseau, because they have infused new dynamics into this word Creole that dates back to the eighteenth century. Thus from a racial, fairly essentialist discourse, we have arrived at a pluri-ethnic concept based on culture, a far more complex notion. Consequently, these writers, prisoners of their class, their education and their ideological inclinations often fall victim to the perils of sanctifying what they imagine to be popular culture while imposing on it a set of rules. They favour and keep artificially alive minority, or frankly outmoded, cultural aspects, believing in all good faith they are giving an authentic picture of their island. As early as 1961, Fanon cautioned those who had difficulty understanding that popular culture is elusive, mobile material: 'Seeking to cling close to the people, he clings merely to a visible veneer. This veneer, however, is merely a reflection of a dense, subterranean life in perpetual renewal.'[42]

It is customary to consider that the three terms—Negritude, Antillanité and now Créolité—are successive manifestations of the quest for identity that led writers to refine the theory of their relationship with a certain idea of culture. I do not share this point of view. For me, Créolité is not just a contemporary concept. It pre-dates Negritude and is destined to outlast it. It was already at work in the *doudouiste* (exotic) authors complacently describing the tropical paradise of their islands and, in so doing, awkwardly expressing the awareness of their difference. It was just as much at work in Michèle Lacrosil as it is in Guy Tirolien and Daniel Maximin, each of whom claim their difference in their own way.

For me it is multiform, plural and polyphonic. It has spoken and continues to speak through the mouth of every Creole writer throughout the ages and wherever the tribulations of life sweep it along.

42 Fanon, *The Wretched of the Earth*, p. 160.